Best Wishes

Charuft Heston

Invention of the Hero

9-30-02

QUEST FOR SURVIVAL

QUEST FOR SURVIVAL

CHARLES J. FLETCHER

Glenbridge Publishing Ltd.

Jacket Illustration
Patricia Hobbs

Published by Glenbridge Publishing Ltd.
19923 E. Long Ave.
Aurora, CO 80016

Library of Congress Catalog Card Number: LC 2001-086271

International Standard Book Number: 0-944435-50-5

Printed in the U.S.A.

10 9 8 7 6 5 4 3 2 1

FOR MY WIFE, HELEN,

OUR TWO SONS,

JEFFREY AND MARK

AND

MY DECEASED PARENTS,

FLORENCE AND HORACE FLETCHER

IN MEMORY OF AIRMEN

Ensign Robert Thomas Burke USNR

Ensign Robert Kenneth Einer USNR

Who lost their lives in a plane crash
at sea on June 22, 1945

As fate would have it, I and Commander G. H. Cagle,

Skipper of Torpedo Squadron Eight, were the only survivors.

Table of Contents

Acknowledgments

*W*hen I began to realize the way my life was progressing as I passed through the incredible period of World War II, I started to appreciate just how lucky I have been. There were striking coincidences, such as my first job in 1941 with Bendix Aviation, helping to manufacture the very components used to fire up the engine of the Grumman Hellcats I flew as a Navy fighter pilot in the Pacific during World War II.

I owe my mechanical and machinist skills to my high school instructor, Horace Houyoux, who recommended me for a position at Bendix Aviation with a letter of recommendation from a local New Jersey Senator, Alfred B. Littell. My teacher and the senator were friends. This was the first real full-time job I ever pursued and was successful in being hired.

Then there was my dad, Horace, who encouraged me to always try to advance my education and strive as best I could to achieve to the fullest, whatever goals I chose to pursue.

While at Bendix Aviation, I could very well have remained a machinist for the rest of my life had it not been for my uncle Ed Bishop, who insisted I try for acceptance into the "Win your Navy Wings of Gold" program. Before doing this, Uncle Ed (my mother's sister's husband) purchased for me several small manuals of algebra, geometry, and physics and literally forced me to prepare for the five-hour exams the Navy required.

After receiving my "Navy Wings of Gold," it was during my advanced fighter pilot training at Vero Beach, Florida, that I became good friends with Wayne (Tex) Collins, who would spend hours in the air with me flying our Hellcats and simulating dog-fighting using our gun cameras instead of bullets. I appreciated his superior flying skills when I would lose a mock battle. Those long hours of practice honed my own aerial combat skills that later allowed me to survive many trials during months at sea during the final days of the Japanese conflict.

Following World War II, during the early part of 1946, my mother, Florence, encouraged me to continue my aeronautical education by attending the Academy of Aeronautics near La Guardia field in New York. During those years of study followed by four years of evening classes at Fairleigh Dickinson University, there were times I felt like throwing in the towel had it not been for Mom and Dad pulling me aside to rearrange my mind so that I could continue through to graduation. In 1951 following my recall back into the Navy, I was given the job as Bureau of Aeronautics Representative (East Coast). At that time Capt. Henry Haselton encouraged me to file for several aeronautical vertical lift airplane and convertaplane patents that we so often discussed during our not so busy office hours. These innovative discussions led me to conceive of the idea of a flying Glidemobile, which later became the first prototype Hovercraft that was successfully demonstrated following my departure from the Navy in 1955. Thanks to my wife, Helen, who spent endless hours typing patent disclosures to help in reducing patent fees I could not afford for my various aeronautical preparations of patent innovations.

Following my return to Reaction Motors Corporation after my Korean War duty in 1955, I had the opportunity to work with several highly educated aeronautical and mechanical rocket engineers who helped me to advance several of my own engineering skills. It was during those years that I had the pleasure of working with Hank Pickering, Hardy Kircher, Raymond Novatny, Vic Adams, and Arthur Brukardt, my immediate boss. Working with such talent helped mold my own ideas of advanced aeronautical concepts that became the stepping-stones leading me to become the founder of Fletch-Aire and subsequently Aerosystems Technology and its current successor, Technology General Corporation (a public company).

During my final years at Reaction Motors, I was again fortunate to meet a number of highly talented individuals who believed in me and agreed to become directors in my company. They were, Rutherford Day, Esq., a Washington attorney; Captain George Robelard, USN, Chief of Patents for the Office of Naval Research; General Jess Larson, founder of the General Services Administration; Robert Lobelson, Editor of *Aero Digest* (and writer of the speech for President John F. Kennedy, used at the inauguration of the new Dulles Airport in Washington, D.C.).

During the early years of our corporate existence, I received expert legal and accounting advice that helped me immensely to overcome early obstacles in my pursuit of corporate development and growth. First it was Bernard Coven, a skilled Securities and Exchange lawyer whose friendship and expertise took my corporation through the rigorous effort of becoming a public company. Also, there was a relatively young attorney, Jay Benenson, who assisted me through early legal problems that seriously threatened our corporate survival. He continues to offer counsel and advice even today. There was Jack Stifelman, CPA, who worked endless hours for little remuneration just to see our corporation begin with a sound financial footing and the advance planning so vital to winning a good banking relationship. Offering financial assistance were Alexander McWilliams, President of McWilliams Forge Company and his banker associate, Charles French, President of the Iron Banks, who had the courage to invest seed money to help me get started in our speculative business venture. I can honestly say that without the assistance of these five friends working for little or no compensation, our company would never have survived to this day, some forty-two years later.

I also want to recognize both my sons, Jeffrey and Mark, for diligently managing their respective corporation divisions (Metaltec and Clawson Machine), being responsible for the success and growth we experienced during the fledgling days of the company.

Finally, thanks to my secretaries, Beverly Murray, Sharon Witkowski and Claudia Simet who spent countless hours typing my difficult-to-read handwritten manuscript.

Introduction

Charles Joseph Fletcher was born December 21, 1922, in the period that produced "The Greatest Generation" — those who lived through the Great Depression of the 1930s and patriotically served their country in World War II, and later in the Korean conflict.

"Chuck" Fletcher, as he's affectionately known, is one of that rare breed of courageous young men who served as naval fighter pilots aboard aircraft carriers during World War II. He returned home, much to his surprise, as a "decorated war hero."

Chuck considers himself a "carefree" but caring individual. He is a modestly tall, lean blond who later was given the nickname of "Flushdeck" for reasons explained later in this story.

Following World War II, he briefly taught school before pursuing his aeronautical interests. In early 1950, he graduated as an aeronautical engineer from the highly regarded Academy of Aeronautics and continued his education at Fairleigh Dickinson University, before pursuing many innovative aeronautical and rocket projects.

With the outbreak of the Korean conflict, Fletcher was called back into active duty while serving as a weekend warrior in a fighter squadron out of New York. It was during this period that he applied his aeronautical skills to invent several vertical lift aircraft concepts, which received recognition in a number of leading aeronautical publications.

From this pioneering work and in preparation for starting his own company after departing from the service for the second time, Fletcher designed and built models of what is now referred to as the famed Hovercraft, plans that he submitted to the U. S. Army. Out of desperation to prove his concept, he quickly sold sufficient stock in his company to his close friends in order to build the first prototype. In the late 1950s, he successfully built and flew the first "inflatable skirt" Hovercraft (which primarily rides on a cushion of air over water) in a demonstration before the editors of *Design News*, a leading technical magazine that awarded him the cover story in 1959.

Early in 1985, the United States Government was sued for $104 million by the British Hovercraft Co., Ltd. for royalties related to the U. S. Government Hovercraft purchases and development in the 1960s, 1970s and 1980s. Subsequently, a young attorney assigned by the U. S. Justice Department, in researching a defense for the government, came upon the Fletcher Hovercraft development story in the United States Library of Congress. This disclosure ultimately became the primary source of evidence to defend the British litigation and, with Fletcher's earlier development work and consultation, was subsequently instrumental in constructing a successful defense for the United States with many news articles and publications making reference to this event.

In 1993, the New Jersey Institute of Technology (formerly Newark College of Engineering/NCE), in harmony with the State of New Jersey, inducted Fletcher into the New Jersey Inventors Hall of Fame and Museum in recognition of his successful development of the now famous "inflatable skirt" Hovercraft. Subsequent honors were received by the recognition of his Hovercraft development in a Discovery Channel television "Wings" documentary.

With changing times in the 1960s and 1970s and a lack of large-scale capital to pursue government interests, Fletcher's businesses expanded rapidly by acquiring stock in a number of companies, setting the stage for a public offering.

Company growth continued until a federal environmental "Superfund" disaster in the 1980s thwarted his drive to greater industrial heights.

Following several successful acquisitions, Fletcher continued to operate his corporate enterprises with focused enthusiasm while in search of significant innovations and financial ventures – all in the face of still pending federal and state litigation over environmental issues that had nothing to do with his parent company. The environmental disaster involved a prior manufacturing firm he had acquired that had buried toxic wastes at the plant site many years before Fletcher had bought the company. Government agencies, however, went after Fletcher's corporate assets to clean up a mess that he had not created.

Fletcher's ongoing battle with government environmental bureaucracies was almost as crucial to his economic survival as his combat duty was to his own survival in World War II and the Korean conflict.

In September 1999 Fletcher's wildest dream came true. He received a letter from the New Jersey Aviation Hall of Fame, informing him that he was selected for induction in the prestigious organization. The dinner ceremony on May 11, 2000, was a long time in coming. For Fletch, the original *Wings Over New Jersey* "ace," he had joined the ranks of the immortals in aviation history.

This is a story of Fletcher's remarkable life from childhood through the war years and his continuing "quest for survival" while developing a fascinating career as an entrepreneur on the cutting edge of technological innovation.

Charles Fletcher's unique story is dedicated to his wife, Helen, who worked through many late nights typing numerous patent applications for his several aeronautical inventions that formed the basis of his company. Her strength and encouragement played a major role in his rewarding and fulfilling life of successes, failures, but always adventures while he was achieving his goal of industrial expansion.

Quest for Survival is a gripping account of one man's journey to overcome daily obstacles while striving through success and despair to achieve ever greater objectives.

But most of all, in Charlie's own words, "It is about asking God's daily help to meet and overcome the challenges of everyday life and then finally realizing one's quest for survival is blessed by a helping hand from God."

Gordon Bishop
Author, Historian, Journalist

Childhood
Recollections

My earliest recollection goes back to the age of four when my dad rented one of the New Jersey Zinc Company houses in the famed fluorescent mineral capital of the world – the little North Jersey zinc mining town of Franklin. This was a place where the zinc company was one of the few places to work. The company owned the house you lived in, as well as the recreational center, the local hospital, and, of course, the company store where your paycheck ended up back with the company you worked so hard for.

The cycle of life was simple. Get up early, go to work, earn enough to pay for your necessities, enjoy a quiet Sunday, then start the week all over again.

Around the age of four, I distinctly remember getting lost on the sidewalk where we lived. All the zinc company houses on our street were alike. At that age I couldn't distinguish one house from another. I had wandered away from our little house and came across some boys playing marbles on the sidewalk. After watching them for a while, I looked up and down the street and didn't know which way to go. Fortunately, a good neighbor, realizing my problem, soon got me back home. Imagine getting lost on the street where you live!

It was not long after that confusing incident that I learned my dad was employed as a stationery engineer, although I did not understand what that was at the time. All I knew was that he worked for the zinc mines. In those days, the company even provided the power plant generators that ran twenty-four hours a day to supply the town's electricity. Dad never could afford a real college education, but he was fortunate to stay out of the mines by going to night school to earn his stationery engineer's license. Although I spent little time with Dad in the early years of my life, I realized just how hard he studied the technical books he bought with whatever pocket change he had and how hard he worked to sustain a strong and close-knit family.

Then one day it happened. After studying over a period of several years in the evenings for his stationery engineering license, Dad finally earned his diploma. How proud he was that day. He never gave up — and was rewarded with what then was the prize of his life. Education paid off for Dad — and his family benefited.

As I later learned from Mom, at the time I was born on the 21st day of December in 1922, the town was under siege with a large-scale epidemic of typhoid fever. My dad was desperately ill and apparently at death's door. Mom later told me that for several weeks, funeral processions passed the house almost every day. Dad, as sick as he was, when told that I had been born, somehow, in his illusory state of mind, envisioned me from his sporadic coma as an Irish Setter. He asked Mom to have a doghouse built for me. There have been times in my life when I actually believed I belonged there, the doghouse, that is. Dogs were an important part of Dad's life. He was an enthusiastic bird hunter and always owned several bird dogs of his own. Mercifully, Dad was one of the few chosen typhoid fever victims who survived the epidemic.

His parents were not so fortunate. Dad's father and mother died early in life, leaving him, at a young age, with heavy responsibilities. Not long after an early marriage to Mom, he was forced to inherit a ready-made family — his three younger brothers, Ben, Leo, and Dick. Dad took in two boarders along the way to supplement his small income to further his education and to make ends meet. Mom, who was better known as "Floss" (short for

Florence), was a gentle, lovable, understanding soul. Dad, on the other hand, was quite temperamental, strict, and determined to maintain a high degree of ethics bound by his strong principles of integrity accompanied by equally strong working principles. For Dad, right was right and wrong could be disastrous. Early in life he taught me that there was only one way. I quickly learned my own balancing act on the tightrope of right or wrong. Being wrong was a sure way to end up with some form of punishment, which usually was either a severe scolding or a typical bottom spanking.

It was several years later when I was first introduced to the subject of mortality. It came at about the age of seven. Dad's brother, Leo, who was still living with us, came down with double pneumonia. Before I realized what was happening an ambulance backed up to our front door and, as I watched intensely, Leo was rushed away on a stretcher. The rear door quickly closed, and the ambulance drove off with lights flashing to the local zinc company hospital. Two days later, Dad told me that Leo had died. Immediately, sadness hung over the household, something I had never before experienced.

As was the custom in the early 1920s, wakes were held in the parlor of the deceased's home. I can still see Uncle Leo laid out in this beautiful wooden box. It was an eerie feeling I will never forget. When the colorful, fragrant flowers arrived, my first realization occurred that someday death would be inevitable. Prior to this event, I had no reason to fully understand that life would someday end. When Dad first let me see Leo lying there so still and peaceful, I couldn't help but think of Leo's active, jovial nature and how he often took sides with me when Dad got on my case for the smallest misbehavior.

Eating was one of them. Somewhere between the ages of six to nine, I had a real hang-up about finishing my meals. I don't know why, but I detested eating. For several years I remained severely underweight and extremely frail, so much so that Mom would take vitamins and wrap them in soft candy for me just to maintain my nutritional level. Being underweight, I soon felt inferior and was often looked down upon by my childhood friends. I specifically remember playing touch football on our front lawn and almost getting killed because I was so skinny.

In the fall of the year, a few of the guys who were five or six years older than I entertained themselves by tossing me into huge piles of leaves as if I were a rubber ball. Also during this impressionable time of my life, these guys, while enjoying our usual cowboy and Indian antics, decided to capture me in their fantasy Indian style. Suddenly, they tied me to a huge tree about five-hundred yards from the back of our house. Before I realized what was happening, Tommy and two of his friends, Frank and Tony, piled a load of dry wood around my feet and quickly set fire to some newspaper before running off and leaving me. Panic-stricken, I screamed to the high heavens as the flames began to lick closer to my legs with no help in sight. Within minutes, one of our neighbors, Mrs. Shauger, a little, gentle old lady who lived next door in our duplex zinc company house, must have heard my screams and came running up over the hill. One of my sneakers was already smoldering and the flames were touching my pants. Mrs. Shauger swiftly stamped out the fire and then untied me. This brave woman most likely saved my life. Those dear friends of mine who had participated in this near massacre will always remain in my memory, a frightening memory at that. Frank became an FBI agent and later a prominent lawyer. Tony was killed in his dad's grocery truck when hit by a car, and Tommy was killed on a motorcycle before the age of sixteen.

Throughout the next several years, I became seriously despondent when it came time to participate in the many competitive school sports. In time, I developed a deep inferiority complex that stayed with me throughout most of my junior high school days. As I approached my junior high school years, several boys who were more physically endowed with muscles and weight began to call me several degrading nicknames. As I look back now, that left a lasting impression on me, causing me much embarrassment, all because of my puny frame. But this childhood bullying ultimately provided the driving force that gave me the determination to overcome any adversity. It also was embedded deep into my mind that if I wanted to survive, I would have to handle future events on my own, no matter how difficult the task became. This imagined "physical handicap" played heavily on my defensive attitude during my youth. For a number of years it caused me to shun developing close friends. I became a loner in defense of my skinny image fantasy. In retrospect, this fantasy was truly blown out of proportion. However, it soon occurred to me why Mom, in maternal desperation, used to force food and vitamins down my throat to keep me from shrinking even further.

It seemed like overnight I developed a strong determination to overcome whatever weight and muscular handicap I possessed. For the next three or so years, I began moderate weightlifting and really became serious about distance swimming. Soon I found myself swimming several miles a day during the summer months when school was out. As exercise became a daily routine, my appetite began to return, and I was convinced I was on the way to recovery from my physically fragile dilemma. As it turned out, I learned that my metabolism was such that at that early age, it made little difference what or how much I ate. There was little physical improvement. A few years later, however, I often looked into the mirror and began to see positive physical effects of the weightlifting, which began to shore up my morale. Then suddenly one day at about the age of fifteen, additional pounds appeared while pursuing my daily weightlifting and swimming regimen. Soon I became the winner of several summer swim races. I knew that my childhood image of inferiority was gone forever. My quest for survival, imagined or real, would forever and continuously become the most dominating challenge of my life.

I soon realized that if I were to improve my attitude about participation in sports, something had to change. So I joined Dad in his favorite outdoor sports, hunting and fishing. The sportsman's relationship with Dad made me realize the high moral principles he had exhibited, and they slowly began to wear off on me. To this day, they have played a critical part in deciding for me the pros and cons of right and wrong. Dad's respect for principles,

Charles J. Fletcher, age 7.

Horace Fletcher

tied to my strong Catholic upbringing, have shaped my life by adhering to the Golden Rule he had set down for me during the formative, growing years of my life.

One characteristic I exhibited shortly after the age of sixteen was my inquisitive interest in new inventions. For a couple of years, I used to gather up all the spare radio parts that I could find around the neighborhood and slowly dismantled them. From these parts, I began putting something original together. For some reason, I began working with a crystal that had been given to me by a close friend. By trial and error, I finally began hearing a faint radio noise being transmitted through the makeshift set. Only God knows how I ever accomplished this small feat with nothing more that a pile of junk radio pieces. For hours I would sit up in my room in the attic and adjust a makeshift aerial while persistently scratching the crystal receiver hoping to pick up the slightest communication through a cheap headset Dad had provided. After several days of adjusting, rewiring, and instinctive crystal scratching, I finally heard my first vocal sound. A distant voice was heard talking about the Depression and suffering people in New York. I became so excited that I ran down two flights of steps to tell Dad and Mom. Having no radio at the time, they were as excited as I was.

Following this interest, I soon became curious about airplanes and found a plan for a model plane in Webb's local newspaper and bookstore. Several months later, after giving up my radio interests, night after night I began experimenting with crazy little rubber band airplane models made of balsa wood and thin tissue paper made of a strong silky substance. When our school week was finished and Saturday came, I would go up to the Franklin High School ball field and attempt to see these aeronautical contraptions take to the air. There were times, believe it or not, when my little rubber band models would fly the length of the field.

Not long after that, I started building gas-powered models. But I soon learned they would fly farther than I could recover them or would crash beyond recognition. I guess I just didn't have the financial resources at that time to keep the hobby going. However, I am sure it was this activity that continued to sustain my interest in aviation to this very day and was certainly the most exciting thing for me during my later teen years.

The many hours I put to work making model planes and fooling around with homebuilt radio sets interfered with my school homework. As a result, my grades during junior high school were generally average at best. That led to the inevitable call from the principal, who invited my dad and me to his office where I was reprimanded for the homework I had failed to turn in. Dad, appreciating my technical capabilities, spared the rod and seemed to understand the situation. He also told me to try to do the very best that I could, never to be discouraged, but to continue and never quit anything I started. This was somewhat contrary to Dad's usual reaction, considering it was a principal scolding me. I think he truly believed I was learning more experimenting with these innovative contraptions than doing those homework assignments. Underneath it all, I could see he liked to tinker around himself.

As I entered my junior high school years, my interest in comprehensive study for the most part was far from my mind and, again, my grades remained borderline passing. Nevertheless, there was one area of strong interest in my final days at high school – and that was in the school's machine shop. When looking back, it probably was one of the best in the school system. Here again my mechanical aptitude stood out as my primary asset. I recall how I just couldn't wait to finish my other classes so I could start the machine shop class. To my surprise, I showed an aptitude for operating a variety of sophisticated machine tools and spent considerable time designing and fabricating a number of small projects. Because of my serious interest, my shop instructor, Mr. Horace Houyoux, took a special liking to me and encouraged me to take on projects far more complex than was intended for the high school class. In short order I reproduced a well-known automatic center punch made up of several small, complicated moving parts. When I finished the project and assembled the unit it worked like a charm. These shop projects, particularly the center punch, which I still have, astound me to this day. In my final year before graduation from high school, I had a compelling desire to pursue the machinist profession. It was here that my interest and desire for creativity became a dominating characteristic of my ambitions.

2

Years Following
High School

*I*n the summer of 1940, soon after graduation, the Big War (as we later called it) started to surface in Europe. Realizing the United States was seriously concerned with the aggressive activities of Adolf Hitler and his German army takeover of Poland, it became apparent that America had to gear up quickly for the manufacture of armaments for both its allies and its own protection.

Being fresh out of high school, I was approached by my shop teacher, Horace V. Houyoux, about my future plans. He asked me if I would be interested in taking a job in the school's machine shop in the evenings to help train those who wanted to learn the trade to serve Uncle Sam's needs. After finishing the course, they would enter the growing work force to meet the demand to build a vast array of military weapons. The offer excited me and soon I began teaching citizens of Franklin, who were much older than I, how to operate a variety of machines I only had begun to master during my final days in high school.

I continued this hands-on instruction for about six months until I learned through newspaper help-wanted ads of the need for qualified machinists to work for the Bendix Aviation Company in Teterboro, New Jersey. I took the opportunity to seek out an interview with a strong recommendation from my beloved instructor (and mentor), Mr. Houyoux. Within days, I was notified that I had been accepted for the position of machinist and soon became trained on some of the most sophisticated precision grinders used to make airplane starters for aircraft being built for World War II. For months on end, I would work the shift from seven in the evening until seven the following morning, six days a week.

During this time, I was living with my uncle, Ed Bishop, in the nearby town of Wyckoff, New Jersey. There were times when I took home a paycheck in excess of $135 a week for my long 12-hour days, 6 days a week. In the early 1940s, that was a substantial amount of money for a kid my age. However, after about seven months of this rigorous routine, I found it seriously cramped my style for the good nightlife and freedom that I began to miss at this youthful age.

As the job began to wear on me, I started looking for something that would replace this daily drudgery. One evening while sitting around the Bendix lunchroom table, one of my supervisors mentioned to me that he had just taken the exams in New York to become a naval aviation cadet to hopefully win his "Navy wings of gold." While inquiring what he had to do to enter this program, I learned about going to Paterson, New Jersey, where I could take five hours of comprehensive tests. Should I successfully complete these exams, then I too, could be sworn in as a naval aviation cadet. I was so charged up by the idea of being a naval cadet that I took a day off and went to Paterson to take the exams. After five hours of attempting to answer every question in just about every high school subject imaginable, many of the questions long and difficult, I was asked to sit in the next room to await the results. Shortly thereafter, a Chief Petty Officer called my name and took me into his private office. Once there, he said, "Sorry son, you just don't have it. You passed a few tests, but failed miserably in algebra." In his own words he told me, "Forget it, kid. You just don't have the substance to be a naval aviator."

Needless to say, I left for home feeling totally heartbroken and dejected and as low as I can remember. It soon dawned on me that I had lost my chance to someday fly the fastest planes in the world.

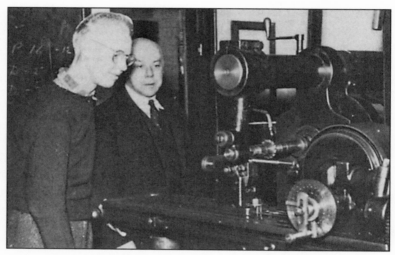

Charles Fletcher at the milling machine under the
watchful eye of supervisor H. V. Houyoux.

The following day when I came home from work and told Uncle Ed what had happened, he immediately said to me that this was not the end of the world. Ed looked me straight in the eye and said, "I'm sure they take these exams in other cities like New York, Boston or Philadelphia, so let's start studying every morning after your twelve-hour shift and schedule a new test somewhere else in a couple of months where they never heard of you."

Whatever my uncle had in mind turned me on because within a few days I had bought algebra, geometry, and physics books on my way home from work.

It wasn't easy, working twelve hours a day. To compensate, I would sneak off the job in the wee hours of the morning at Bendix or catch a few winks while sitting on the commode. This gave me enough energy after arriving home in Wyckoff to complete a few hours of study on my own. Then a short sleep and it was off to work again.

For the next three months, Uncle Ed tutored me by asking questions and encouraging me to keep up the study until I was ready to drop. Finally one day Uncle Ed said to me that next Monday he was going to drive me over to 120 Broadway in New York City since he had heard that they were giving tests for naval aviators, and he believed I had a chance to make it. After what seemed to be endless anxiety and sleepless nights, Monday came and Uncle Ed and I jumped into his antique Rio and we drove off to Manhattan.

Arriving at the test site, a lump larger than an apple choked my throat, and I physically feared getting out of the car. Uncle Ed, being the great guy that he was, instantly gave me a confidence-building pep talk and assured me over and over again that I was as smart as any of the others going in for these tests.

Alas, bidding Uncle Ed farewell, I marched into the building and was directed to the elevators where I ended up on the 20th floor. It was my fateful moment of truth. For me, this was it. I had to make it!

I checked in and joined a group of some thirty-four applicants in a room with a school-like atmosphere. I was hoping I wouldn't see the Chief Petty Officer who had given me the bad news in Paterson and who might say, "What the hell are you doing here since you failed once before?"

Soon the tests were passed out, instructions were given, and once again I found myself sweating profusely. Almost five hours later, I completed the last series of questions, just hoping and praying I had done better than that Paterson episode. When I finished the tests, I did not have the slightest notion what the outcome would be. When it was over, a chief directed all of us out into another room, as I had previously experienced in Paterson. There we sat for what I thought was the rest of my life until finally a Lieutenant Commander entered the room and said, "All of you, when I call your names, please step into the adjacent room." Then came the names, one by one. As the names were called, I began to shudder at the possibility that I again had failed. As the group got smaller and smaller, there were about 15 of us remaining out of the original group of about 34. Still my name had not been called. As the last few names were called, there were 12 of us left. And as he looked each of us over, we all sensed that we were the ones who had failed. Soon the Commander closed the room door behind us and, for sure, I died a thousand deaths just sitting there waiting for further instructions. About five minutes later, the Lieutenant Commander returned, looked us over with a long pause and said, "Congratulations. You boys are the successful candidates."

I leaped from my chair with joy. Then the Commander cautioned us and said that these tests were only the beginning of the process. That said, he offered to put us up for the evening at a nearby hotel only to return the next day to undergo the rigorous physical exams in store for us.

The following day, starting at 8 a.m., the testing began: eyes, ears, nose, throat, physical structure, feet, weight, stability tests, you name it. I vividly remember the one where they sit you in a swirling chair, blindfolded, and spin your brains out for about a minute to check your equilibrium. When I became awfully dizzy, I was sure I had failed. Contrary to my belief, it only meant that my internal ear gyros were working correctly and that was the way it was supposed to be.

Finally the results of the physical tests were in. Again we were subjected to another calling of our names. This time, my name was called among several of the other twelve candidates remaining. As it turned out, two of the twelve had failed the physical. Again, I was elated and excited that I had made it this far. At that point, the remaining ten, including myself, were invited to lunch only to return for what we did not expect: a final applicant review.

We were taken to a new room where there were three offices in front of our seats with signs (A), (B), and (C). Each office had a Lieutenant or Lieutenant Commander ready to conduct a comprehensive interview. I thought to myself, "What if I failed now? I would never be able to live with myself."

One by one, we entered Room A where the interrogation reached back to the days of my childhood. Then Room B and finally Room C, where I remembered specific questions like, "Did I ever hate my mother? Did I ever smash up a car? Was I always ready to defend myself if a fight started? Why was I here in the first place?"

After thirty minutes of this grilling, seven of us emerged and were sent to a room where a podium was in place with a large picture of a naval aviator sitting in the cockpit of his fighter plane with the bold caption "Win Your 'Navy Wings of Gold' " depicting an oversized picture of the Navy's impressive gold wings.

In short order, a commander took charge and crisply announced: "Gentlemen, you have been selected as a chosen few for being one of the Navy's potential 'cream of the crop.' You have just completed one of the most extensive and grueling mental and physical tests ever devised."

After a few minutes, a commander arrived in his slick Navy blues adorned with his scrambled eggs atop his hat and, of course, his shiny gold wings. He was without a doubt the envy of all of us.

"Gentlemen," he proclaimed sharply, "this country is at war with the Japanese, and you, gentlemen . . . you are going to represent the cornerstone in turning this conflict around."

Taking a deep breath, he continued: "Many of you passing through here today may never see the end of this conflict, but rest assured, each of you will be a glorious part of the deterring force that will ultimately bring Japan to its knees."

Ending with that dramatic declaration, the commander then ordered us to "rise and be sworn in as Naval Aviation Cadets."

As our enlistment papers were being passed out, those of us who survived this two-day mental, physical, and personal challenge congratulated each other before heading for home. Having no idea how I was going to leave New York, I asked about a bus schedule, which would get me back to my Uncle Ed's place across the Hudson River to Wyckoff, New Jersey.

I will never forget the look on my Uncle Ed's face when he learned I was a full-fledged Naval Aviation Cadet. There is no question in my mind that it was Uncle Ed who pressed me into believing in myself to pass those difficult exams. Uncle Ed (who married my mom's sister, Freda) was a man of great vision who, I guess, never really accomplished in life the success of which he had dreamed. As I recalled from my early childhood, Uncle Ed always wanted to be his own boss and explored several businesses with the hope of reaching a fast pot of gold. I remember him selling fruits, vegetables, cheese and other delights from a truck door-to-door. Later he ran his own butcher shop and God knows what else. Uncle Ed even invented a new car wax, which sold well and was an excellent polish. It was so successful at the time that he bought a substantial home in the heart of Wyckoff. Nevertheless, Uncle Ed was the one person whose dreams of success opened my eyes and ultimately contributed to my own successful career.

Uncle Ed was dynamic, full of energy, and always hoping for the one thing that would make him financially successful. Dear Ed was really one of a kind. Without warning, he died suddenly at the age of forty-five. A fatal heart attack ended his life in his prime while he was still struggling to start a new business as a wholesale/retail tire manufacturer and distributor. Was this the project that would have made him his fortune and allowed him a life of adventure to pursue any interesting idea he wished?

Uncle Ed had three children: "Dode" (short for Dolores), Ed, Jr., and Gordon. Although I knew each well, I became more

Uncle Ed Bishop and Fletcher after winning
his "Wings of Gold."

attached to Gordon, probably because he used to admire me as a naval aviator. As it turned out over the years, Ed, Jr. in many ways patterned himself after his father – moving from one business to the another, mostly building custom homes and additions to homes.

Gordon, on the other hand, always had an inner desire for achievement by driving himself beyond expectations. Gordon, who is our closest relative on my mom's side, is today an extremely successful man. Finishing college at Rutgers University by working days and going to classes at night on a newspaper scholarship, Gordon specialized in the field of writing. He was (until 1996) a leading editorial writer for the Newark *Star-Ledger*, New Jersey's largest newspaper, where he gained international renown for his work as an environmental award-winning investigative reporter and columnist. He was the recipient of more than a dozen national and fifteen state journalism awards, becoming New Jersey's first "Journalist of the Year" in 1986 and the only unprecedented five-time consecutive winner of the Scripps-Howard Foundation Conservation Award and four-time winner of the New Jersey Society of Professional Journalists Distinguished Public Service Award, including six first-place awards by the New Jersey Press Association. He also received eight Congressional Commendations for his pioneering work as a journalist in the 1970s, 1980s, and 1990s. He has authored several books and has written and hosted more than 100 television programs.

Working with Uncle Ed and living with his family became the kickoff point of my career in general aviation.

Within a couple of weeks after being sworn into the Navy, I quit my job and returned home to Franklin, where I waited daily for those orders that would send me off to an unknown college for cadet training. While several weeks passed, a few close friends and I continued to study mathematics and physics in preparation for our college assignments. Between times, we would meet at the local high school gym to lift weights and box with each other in an effort to remain physically trim. This later proved to be a real asset in dealing with my Navy physical training activities.

3

The Beginning of My Naval Career at Baylor University

*O*ne morning while I was oversleeping, Mom came running into the bedroom with that anxiously awaited letter from the Navy Department. Sure enough, this was it. The letter directed me to leave immediately for Baylor University in Waco, Texas, via New York City, where I would join others cadets.

I packed with excitement and bid Mom farewell. Dad drove me into New York to meet the delegation preparing to leave. I knew Dad was proud of me, but he was never one to show his emotions. Arriving in New York, Dad gave me one last hug and a handshake before leaving for home.

Just before getting ready to leave New York by train on a cold January day in 1943, someone said the trip would be delayed because the train scheduled for us was quarantined because several travelers had come down with scarlet fever. As the afternoon dragged on, a second train pulled into Grand Central Station, but somehow it didn't seem as classy as the first train. After boarding, it became apparent that there were no sleepers, and the seats were hard and uncomfortable. This "cattle car," as it soon became known, gave us a wild ride to Waco, Texas. It was so bad that black smoke from the engine would pour into the windows from time to time, getting soot all over our hands and faces. Since there was little else to do, I slowly became acquainted with the rest of the cadets who spent considerable time during the three-day trip singing the great songs of World Wars I and II – "Yankee Doodle Dandy," "Grand Ole Flag," and many others. Although I was never really one for carrying a tune, it did help keep my patriotic spirit up throughout this miserable, dirty trip.

As we approached the South and later Texas, it was a pleasant feeling to experience the warm change in climate. Never being that far away from home, this long and tiresome trip was a whole new experience. After what seemed like an eternity of "clickity-clacks" on the railroad tracks, we arrived in Waco on a nice warm sunny day, and we were glad to stretch our legs. Tired and filthy from the smelly and sweaty trip through the south, we couldn't wait to see our new home at Baylor University.

As we left the train, a short, skinny fellow with a derby appeared and quickly introduced himself as the college's cadet coordinator during our stay at the university. At the school, we were rapidly assigned a room in one of their little dormitories where we settled in for what was to become a comprehensive academic program for half the day, followed by flight training the second half. I can remember that first night, lying awake in the dark with the anxiety of anticipating my first flying lesson.

That morning our coordinator, "Little Caesar," as he came to be known, led us to a nearby classroom for our first lecture. Placing his derby on the podium, he began telling us what to expect during our stay. Following his brief introduction and telling us a bit about the renowned Baylor University, he immediately informed us that this part of our training was no child's play and that within a short three-month period, 25 percent of this class of approximately thirty-four students would be washed out of the program and sent on to the Great Lakes Naval Training Station in Chicago for further assignment. The realization of what I was in for to stay in the program sent icy shivers up and down my spine. I kept thinking, "What if I failed math? What if I failed physics? What if I failed flight training?" I would never be able to explain my failure to Mom and Dad, not to mention Uncle Ed, who was my inspiration to apply for naval aviation training in the first place. It was then and there that I told myself that I would do everything in my power to make it work. I just knew that once I started to fly, I would love it beyond all expectations.

As we settled in and it came time for us to depart for the nearby airport, I could hear my heart thumping heavily in my chest. Soon a bus drove up and we were off to the airport. When we arrived, we were split into groups of three and assigned an instructor for the duration of the flight program. My instructor, a fellow by the name of Darren, with a typical Texas twang, introduced himself and explained the program. After several brief lectures, Darren led me out to his Piper Cub two-seater and told me to get in. Taxiing the plane to the end of the field, Darren said, "This is where we find out what the hell you're made of." I didn't know what he meant at the time. Darren opened the throttle and started the takeoff roll. I don't believe we were 300 feet in the air when he said, "You got it." Half-scared to death, I grabbed the stick and began getting my first feel of an airplane in flight. As I began moving the stick, the plane would rise sharply and roll from side to side with the slightest movement. "Fletch," he barked, "You have to handle that stick like a bear cub handles his dick. Nice and gentle. If you don't, it will kick you in the teeth."

Climbing up to around 5,000 feet, Instructor Darren, with me on the dual controls, began making our first full circles without losing altitude. Then came "S" turns to develop my coordination, then my first introduction into a full stall spin. WOW! What excitement as we pulled the nose of the Cub up to the sky. With the throttle off, Darren pushed the left rudder to the floor and before I knew what was happening, the wing snapped over to the left and the plane was spinning straight downward as I watched the ground coming straight up at me, spinning out of control like a drunken fool. Suddenly, as the stick snapped forward and the rudders became neutral, the spin came to a halt while the nose slowly came up and the sky became visible once more. As the recovery of pulling out of this dive began to drain the blood from my head, I had just learned what blacking out really meant.

After landing back at the airport, Darren was kind enough to tell me I had handled the plane as well as could be expected for the first time, and if things went well for the next eight hours, I'd be ready to solo. Just the thought of being in that spin alone triggered a cold sweat across my brow.

For the next several days, it became somewhat routine. Leave for the airport, get a two-hour lesson, then back to the Baylor campus for four hours of serious academic training. After about my sixth hour of flight training, I began to sense I was on a learning curve that went straight up like a plane climbing vertically to the heavens. This became apparent when Darren asked me to execute a full two-turn spin left, then right, trying to stop rotation on a dime. While never really praising my efforts, Darren seemed to be pleased with my skills and my sincere interest in asking questions I couldn't answer for myself.

One day while taxiing out to take off with Darren, we arrived at the takeoff end when all of a sudden he announced, "Fletch, in one minute this plane is all yours. You are going to solo." With a dry lump in my throat, I couldn't believe what he was saying until he unstrapped himself and proceeded to depart from the plane. The witching hour had come unexpectedly. After a few last-minute instructions, Darren closed the cabin door and pointed for me to go.

God, what excitement! My heart raced furiously while my whole body trembled. Taking a deep breath, I pushed the throttle forward as I was trained to do, and lo and behold, as I slowly applied back pressure to the stick, I leaped into the air and began flying solo for the first time! As I climbed up to my specified altitude of 6,000 feet, I couldn't help but feel the exhilaration of freedom of flight. What an indescribable, delirious sensation, like you would somehow expect after dying and going to heaven!

As the flight progressed, I made bolder and steeper turns until I finally felt that I was the master of my own fate. When I arrived safely back and made that first solo landing on my own, Darren met me at the plane and said, "Now the hard part starts." Over the next several weeks, Darren put me through a variety of complex maneuvers, emergency landing procedures and more spins, including a preliminary introduction to aerobatics.

After our eleventh week, word was out that six of our class failed to pass flying for one reason or another. A few just couldn't handle the fright from spins or even solo flight. Darren approached me and said he was proud of the way I responded to his training, and that if I kept up the good work, I would eventually win those coveted but elusive "Navy Wings of Gold."

There still remained one more challenge to my survival at Baylor, and that was the final academic tests to be given by "Little Caesar." Realizing I was doing well with flying, I stayed up for the next several nights until well after four in the morning just studying for the final exam. I was really scared to death of exams. Never did I feel confident enough to be certain that I would pass.

On the Saturday before departing Baylor, we met in "Little Caesar's" classroom and proceeded to take tests from early morning to well past noon. Shortly after, the term grades were posted in the dorm. Hearing that the scores were posted, I rushed down to get the final results, scanning the list until I came to my name. There it was. I had passed all the tests but only marginally so for Naval History.

I soon realized another nine students failed these tests and would be sent up to the Great Lakes Naval Air Station for other noncommissioned officer assignments. God forbid if this ever happened to me! I probably would never have accomplished another thing as long as I lived. Thinking back to when we had first arrived at Baylor, I remembered what "Little Caesar" had said: "Before this phase of the course is over, many of you will have failed." After hearing that statement, I asked myself, "Didn't Jesus say something like that at the Last Supper?"

Pre-flight class at Baylor University, December 1942 (Fletcher, arrow, Darren, our instructor, bottom row, second from right.)

4

Training at the University of Georgia

*T*he day finally arrived when we again departed by train. This time I learned that I was assigned to preflight training at the University of Georgia in Athens.

As the trip to Athens progressed, word got out that the physical training program there was brutal at best, and although this phase involved no flying, it was designed to toughen you up before continuing in your training program. Little did I know at the time what severe discipline was to be imposed on us. This was really our first introduction to comprehensive military training by first-class athletic directors using every tool in their arsenal in an effort to break us down both physically and mentally.

Each day started promptly at 6 a. m. with a shrill bugle call followed by five minutes to make up your bed, shower, shave, comb your hair, and be ready for daily inspection in platoon formation. Being late by as little as five seconds would draw demerit points which, if accumulated in excess of fifty, would be automatic cause for being expelled from the program. As I discovered, points were dished out at the drop of a hat. You would never know what criteria they would use during their early morning inspections.

I can still picture the drill sergeant passing rigidly through the dorm, looking intensely at the way each of us made our bed. Every once in a while, he would stop at a particular bed and toss a shiny penny on top of the sheet. If for some reason this penny did not bounce into the air, he would rip the bed apart from top to bottom with a penalty of five points coupled with an assignment of walking fifty yards back and forth with fifty pounds of sand strapped to your back, plus parading with a rifle for a period of one hour.

One particular morning after the bugle blew reveille, I somehow became slightly detained, so I skipped shaving, thinking my light blond peach fuzz would never be detected by "ole eagle eyes." As I stood there at attention as rigid as I could be, staring straight ahead, I began seeing this heartless bastard of a drill sergeant slowly approaching out of the corner of my left eye. As he approached me, he stopped dead in his tracks, looked down at my shiny boots and said, "Cadet, your shoes are beautifully shined, so much so that I can see a reflection in them that tells me you forgot to shave." How he knew, I will never know. "Cadet," he snapped, "that will cost you five demerits and a one-hour march." Let me tell you that a one-hour march at a military pace with a fifty-pound sack of sand on your back made your legs feel like rubber bands after the first half-hour. At the end of this ordeal, I struggled back to the barracks and collapsed on my cot.

This program was set up to be physically cruel. After breakfast at 6:30, the platoon sergeant marched us double-time across a deep ravine to the other end of the campus where the university gyms were located. This three-quarter of a mile high-speed walk up one hill and down the other every day of the week soon developed leg muscles as hard as steel. Then after two hours of comprehensive gymnastics, it was back to the dorm, double-time, where lunch was served. After lunch, we swiftly departed again for class, where for the next three hours aeronautical studies were thrust upon us to a point of mind-numbing exhaustion. Then studying started at 6 p. m. followed by taps at 10 p.m. sharp.

As the program progressed, word got around about the competition boxing we were scheduled to do during the last week of our training. By this time, if you were still in the program, you can bet you were in the best of shape. Much too soon the day arrived for competitive boxing. As we arrived at the gym, I became curious who I would box. We found out right away. We were ordered to form two lines and proceeded to march into the gym. Then, with an order of "Line A, Right Face" and "Line B, Left Face," the next thing you knew, the guy you faced was the guy you boxed for three, two-minute rounds. As I looked at the guy in front of me, I tried desperately to size him up. It didn't matter if he was 6'2" at 195 pounds or 5'8" at 140 pounds. That was the guy you had to fight. Refuse and you were out of the program. Quit boxing short of a knockout and you were also out of the program. Fortunately for me, my opponent was only slightly taller than I, but I knew that could be deceiving.

Eventually, my turn came. The gong sounded and I slowly pranced around. After three grueling rounds and a couple of swollen eyes, I ended this conflict proud of the fact that I had lasted through the last round. After I got back to the barracks, my roommate told me that the guy I had fought had trained for six months as a "Golden Glover." Although I lost the fight on points, I made the grade in this unpredictable event. By the time I finished this program three months later, I was as fit as a fiddle, cocky, and ready to take on the world.

After a brief graduation ceremony at the University of Georgia, we were each given a new set of orders, which, in my case, directed me to report to the Naval Air Station in Olathe, Kansas, following a two-week leave. With the worst behind me, or so I thought, I grabbed a commercial plane for New Jersey and arrived home all decked out in my flashy navy blue cadet uniform. In the little town of Franklin, believe me, it was hot stuff to be a Naval Aviation Cadet. Mom and Dad were so proud that I had succeeded to this point in training that Mom cooked one of her big, family-favorite roast beef dinners just for me.

5

Preflight Training

*B*efore I could get to relax on this brief vacation at home, it was time to leave for Olathe, Kansas. Olathe was then a small town some sixty miles west of Kansas City that had its own Navy preliminary flight training school. Long before I arrived in Olathe, I was warned that this would be a comprehensive flight-training phase in the legendary "Yellow Pearl," a bi-wing trainer that really gave you a workout in preparation for advanced flight training.

At Olathe, we were again assigned an instructor whose responsibility was to teach you all the advanced maneuvers and later aerobatics, which was also designed to weed out the men from the boys on a more competitive level. Here the program was broken down into several phases of instruction, each of which provided a final check ride with an unknown instructor. After these check rides, it was customary for the instructor, who generally sat in the front seat, to point his thumb either up for passing or down for failing. Failing any one of these check rides automatically meant you had to appear behind closed doors before a board of officer pilots who discussed your area of deficiency. It was here they decided to either give you another check ride or dismiss you from the program immediately. Generally, unless you really were awful, they would give you at least one more chance.

One of the more precision maneuvers was to cut power at 500 feet directly opposite from where you intended to emergency land, then vary your glide path through whatever means possible to make your landing within a 30-foot circle. This was no easy task, even for the most competent pilots, if the wind was strong and variable as it sometimes is in Kansas. Five hits out of seven tries were necessary to pass this test on the final check ride.

Everything had been going along just fine until I was scheduled for this test. On that day, the wind was excessively gusty, 10 miles an hour one minute and 25 miles an hour the next. Sure enough, I only hit four out of the seven and wondered on the way back if the instructor would pass me because of the unusually rough wind. As the propeller coasted to a halt, the instructor lifted his arm and pointed his thumb down, which stunned me for the first time, knocking the wind right out of me. I knew right there that my career was in jeopardy. Walking back to the hanger with my big parachute bundle drooping behind me, the instructor said that my flight was marginal and he felt that with another week's training, I might be ready to take another test if the board approved it at my hearing. For me, this was a scary time in my career.

The following day I was scheduled for the Board Review and, never having had one before, I was petrified. I was called into the Board Room and asked to sit across from six directors made up of the instructor staff to hear my case. Their review of my progress, they noted, had been excellent, except for this test. As a result, the Board recommended a retest within a week.

For the next four days, I solo practiced the "emergency dead-engine spot landing" until I was satisfied I could hit seven out of seven, each accomplished by precision judgment of my flight position, slipping and sliding back and forth to regulate my glide path until I was sure the wheels would land precisely in the prescribed circle. Now that I look back on these events, I realize how important this precise judgment training is to polish your coordination should an emergency require you to land powerless in a chosen predetermined area, many times making the difference between life or death, as we later often learned from reported situations.

On the following Monday, my instructor took me out to the test field where I proceeded to meet each landing with precision. One after one, each landing was perfect – seven out of seven. Before we ever returned to the field, my instructor raised his arm and pointed his thumb skyward. With a sigh of relief, I headed to my home base to be greeted by the rest of the instructor group, all of whom congratulated me.

As was the custom, I was then assigned a new instructor who was a young and cocky lieutenant, not the type to let you think for one moment that you were a special student who deserved his kindness. No, this guy was dead serious and down-right mean. I knew immediately I was in for a tough time. I just hoped I would not lose my cool long enough to have him cancel my cadet status.

The one single thing that stood out about this guy was the way we started each training flight. Typically, we would slip into our seat parachute, and I would climb into the rear seat of the famed Yellow Pearl, hook up our intercom hearing tube, and start the rollout. Never a word would be spoken as we taxied out to the takeoff position. As we completed checking the mags, a simple way to determine just how functionally sound the engine was running, my new instructor would say in a harsh voice, "Take this crate up to 10,000 feet and when I tell you, pull the nose straight up in the air, kick the damn left rudder, shove that stick full forward, leave it there and stall this son of a bitch . . . Oh, yeah, once we start inverted spinning, don't do a thing until I tell you to recover."

This, frankly, was the one thing I remember that really scared the living daylights out of me. As we entered a vicious inverted spin, it seemed the earth was coming up at us a mile a minute, all the while the violent spinning would cause your equilibrium to go into total disorientation; it seemed like an endless trip to our death, spin after spin after spin, with the centrifugal force of an inverted spin literally throwing us out of the cockpit while at the same time glancing at the altimeter periodically watching our altitude diminishing and ground closing fast.

At last, a shrieking voice from this hard-nosed instructor bellowed over the intercom, "Snap it out! Snap it out!" With my efforts failing to break out of the spin, he yelled in a screaming voice, "I got it!" I got it! "Give me the damn stick!"

WOW! What a ride! This craft was wound up so tight that by the time we completed six or eight full revolutions, it would take the power of a gorilla to break the stall and recover. Those spins were so lengthy and violent that being in the back seat you would see the wacky guy's neck turn bright red as the centrifugal force rushed the blood into his brainless head.

After about two weeks of this daily routine, one particular spin almost became unmanageable. As the spin recovered from the left, a new stall occurred and the spin started violently to the right. By the grace of God alone, my instructor, not me, was able to recover just in time to pull out a little more than tree level height from a beginning altitude of just over 10,000 feet. Looking back, I believe to this day that this spin taught him a lesson, because during the next flight he canceled this abnormal spin event. At one point, I really thought he was losing his marbles, or was even perhaps suicidal.

Fortunately for me, this irresponsible instructor had received a severe sunburn while falling asleep at a local pool. As a result, the command reassigned me to another instructor. I had a hard time holding back my joy and relief. After this brief episode of daily fear, I was sure nothing would ever frighten me again.

With a new instructor, I was thankful to have a guy with skill and common sense. I quickly progressed through the complex aerobatics stage doing everything from snap rolls to Cuban eights. This was a period in my training when I had, for the first time, that glorious feeling of flying confidence so necessary to go to the limit to become a naval fighter pilot.

By the second month of this rigorous daily ritual, I began to get real confident in my ability to fly, just the thing that can get you into real trouble should an unexpected emergency arise. Instinctively, I realized my exposure to overconfidence and continued the program to completion with caution and great personal satisfaction.

Following a few weeks of comprehensive cross-country training, we finally reached a point of capability that dictated our ultimate assignment with the Navy. As I had hoped from the beginning, I was given a high grade of flying efficiency and was recommended for advanced fighter training at Corpus Christi, Texas.

6

Advanced
Fighter Training

Soon after arriving at Corpus Christi, I was assigned to an advanced fighter training class. This was the ultimate challenge — refining and honing my aeronautical skills. It included day and night formation flying, comprehensive aerobatics, instrument training, and a complex series of supporting aerobatic programs in a four-plane formation.

During the final days at Corpus Christi, we were checked out in the renowned North American AT-6, a fighter trainer, preceding assignment to the ultimate "Hellcat" — the best carrier-based fighter the Navy had at the time.

As the days of advanced training ended, we developed high-speed combat skills doing overhead vertical-dive firing runs at airborne "sleeves" being towed by another plane. The fabric sleeve resembles a cone, approximately thirty feet long with a three-foot diameter circle. When we shot at the sleeve, it left bullet holes, or colored markings, revealing our level of marksmanship. These straight-down dive firing runs sharpened our skills in the art of preliminary dogfighting. Mixed in with this was a short spurt of dive-bombing using small smokebombs that we would release from a plunging dive at 10,000 feet onto a thirty-foot bulls-eye painted on the ground.

The training that clearly left an impression on me was the rapid transition in air speed from the bi-wing "Yellow Pearl" we

flew at Olathe, Kansas, to the high-speed aerobatics in close formation, an on-the-edge thrill beyond description.

It all came to an end much too fast – faster, I felt, than our
planes at full throttle. One day the base Admiral summoned our
surviving class members and, with an impressive military band
and short parade, we gathered in front of a rather large stand lined
with a number of special guests and dignitaries to become full-
fledged naval officers and to be honored with receiving our precious "Navy Wings of Gold."

The highlight of the ceremony was a dynamic speech by the
now well-known Capt. Joe Foss, the marine aviator who had
made numerous fighter kills in early Pacific engagements. Joe
Foss was a handsome devil who reminded me of the swashbuck-
ling movie star, Errol Flynn.

As the ceremony unwound and the awards were handed out,
I heard the name Ensign Charles J. Fletcher blast from the podium
speaker. What a thrill this was to be a full-fledged Naval aviator,
a member of the *crème de la crème*, as "Wings of Gold" aviators
were often referred to, yet still very green and ready to accept
whatever lay ahead. I can truly say that this was the proudest day
of my life. And I was only twenty, not yet old enough to vote. If
only Uncle Ed could have been there to witness this event.

With my flight training completed, I immediately took
advantage of my two-week leave before accepting my new
assignment at the advanced day and night fighter base in Vero
Beach, Florida.

After leaving Corpus Christi by bus for Dallas, I found my
way to Love Field, Texas, in hopes of bumming a ride on an Army
B-25 bomber heading east. As luck would have it, I was invited
to join a couple of Army pilots who were headed out to Mitchell
Field, New York. This was my first experience flying in an Army
bomber. As we flew across the country, I was given an opportunity to take the copilot's seat and experience the thrill of control-
ling, for a brief period, one of the Army's most successful bomber
warbirds. What I especially remember about that trip was making
a mild left and right turn while on full instruments. Just moving

the control wheel left and right was like maneuvering a Mack truck. I realized how lucky I was to be able to fly advanced fighters that would turn on a dime with the slightest movement of the stick and rudder controls. This brief experience was just another rare moment in the evolution of my flight career.

After arriving at New York's Mitchell Field, I hopped on a bus to Newark, New Jersey, then finally back to that rural country zinc-mining town of Franklin, my roots, and where I still run a technology company with several subsidiaries. On the way home, I was fortunate to hitch a short ride with one of the town locals. When I reached home that early, cold, wintry February morning, Dad was just getting up when I opened the door yelling as loud as I could, "I'm home!" What a joyous welcome it was. Mom was so proud of my sharp Navy blues officer uniform with the shining gold braid ensign stripes and, most of all, my "Navy Wings of Gold." Within minutes, Dad just had to snap a dozen or so pictures to memorialize the return of his son.

After a brief celebration and short visit with nearby neighbors, I had to catch a few winks of sleep. After all, I had been up almost forty-eight hours hitchhiking from Corpus Christi, Texas, via several modes of air and bus transportation. Suddenly, I was totally exhausted. Only the thrill of this graduation experience kept me on my feet for that long and arduous trek from the Lone Star State to the Garden State.

After getting back my strength with a couple of hours of sleep and a good hot shower, I did what every red-blooded American boy did upon arriving home on leave: I called an old girlfriend who lived just down the road. Irene was an attractive gal and I certainly had a schoolboy crush on her and wanted to see her before departing for Vero Beach Naval Air Station. Happily, I found she was home, and she agreed to be my date for the evening. What a night it would be. With my Dad's 1940 Chevrolet, which I called the "Blue Beetle," I cruised over to her house to pick her up and proceeded to the nearby movie house. Franklin had little to offer in entertainment, so that seemed the logical choice. Following the show, which I cannot recall, we decided to drive out of town about twelve miles to a nice little tavern built on the side of a lake. There in the dim lights of a secluded booth, we reminisced about our earlier school days and danced the evening away with popular 1940s tunes until well past midnight. I remember the last words the bartender said as we were leaving: "Drive carefully, son, you look a bit tired."

We rode home slowly and carefully, Irene falling asleep on my shoulder. As we approached Franklin, I suddenly heard a half-dozen sharp bangs and felt a clanking jolt as the car plunged over a bank and came to a loud halt. I had fallen asleep at the wheel of Dad's Chevy. Luckily the car had only sheared a few fence posts before coming to a crunching stop. All I could remember was waking up. How I ever missed two telephone poles, I'll never know. Irene looked at me and I looked at her, wondering what had happened. Neither of us was hurt, but the engine was damaged because the radiator was blowing hot steam everywhere. I knew I was going to be in deep trouble when Dad found out. It was his car, so I had to move fast.

Once again, luck was on my side. I had an Uncle, "Bub" Romyns (my mother's brother) whom I thought I could call at that wee hour of the morning for help. Irene and I decided to abandon the car and walk on a nearby railroad track for about three miles since it passed near our homes. I guess I woke Uncle Bub at about 3:30 a.m. and explained the circumstances about Dad's car. I simply didn't have the nerve to tell Dad first. He surely wasn't the kind of guy who would take it lightly, particularly since cars were scarce because of the war, as were auto repair parts.

Nevertheless, Uncle Bub agreed to drive me back to the car, which we had abandoned over a road bank. Looking over the situation, he went over to see a friend who owned a garage and a wrecker truck. With the help of Uncle Bub's friend and his wrecker, we were able to extract the "Blue Beetle" Chevy from the swamp before dawn.

At about 5:30 a.m., I arrived back home and sneaked into bed without awakening Dad. Sometime around 8:30 a.m. or so, I heard a knock on my bedroom door. It was Dad, demanding to know where his Chevy was. When I told him what had happened, I thought all hell would break loose. Within an hour or so, Dad quieted down long enough to realize his favorite son of the day was alive and well. Although the car was in need of serious repair, he agreed he would get it fixed. I realized that here I was home for less than forty-eight hours and already I had wiped out the old man's only car with nothing to replace it for months to come.

7

Combat Tactics

*B*efore the end of my two week leave, orders came by telegram for me to report to Vero Beach Naval Air Station as soon as possible. Over the next three months, I underwent the most aggressive aerial combat training in the Navy's now famous "Hellcat" fighter, which had just arrived from the production lines of Grumman Aircraft Company. Within a week, I became fully oriented with the controls of the Hellcat. That first flight was nerve-racking. As a single-seat fighter, there was no one with you to bolster your courage. You had to rely on blind faith (sheer guts and nerves) to get in the Hellcat and taxi out to the runway for that first takeoff in this unforgiving fighter. This machine would literally leap off the ground and climb to 15,000 feet in minutes. At that elevation, the use of oxygen masks was a new experience to me.

There were several weeks of aerial thrills with scheduled dogfights using gun cameras instead of real bullets, then high speed dives firing real 50 caliber bullets at a towed canvas sleeve. In less than ten short weeks, we became advanced Navy fighter pilots complete with tight formation, flying day and night, making hundreds of practice land-based carrier landings, and flying this state-of-the-art fighter hanging off the prop at air speeds slightly more than 70 knots. This extremely controlled slow speed flight was what distinguished a naval aviator from our competing Army pilots.

Having to land aboard an aircraft carrier with possible high winds and rough seas, which can cause the stern to pitch up and down as much as fifty or so feet, required the most comprehensive skill a Navy pilot could muster. In the early 1940s, a new Hellcat probably cost upwards of $600,000. Not a lot by today's standards, but a royal mint then. Consequently, Uncle Sam took the accidental destruction of a new fighter seriously.

During my brief stay at Vero Beach, Florida, I became close to a half dozen great guys, but especially Ensign Wayne Collins, a Texas lad who was as dapper as movie idol John Wayne. "Tex," as we called him, actually participated in a 1940 rodeo in New York's Madison Square Garden. He could ride those steers like a veteran cowboy. Tex, with his long lean frame, had a stomach as hard as a rock from punching those steers. When it came to dogfighting, Tex and I both had the kill-or-be-killed instinct, which had been drummed into our heads from the early days of our training at Athens, Georgia.

Every day Tex and I would jump into our hot new Hellcats and climb up to 15,000 feet, wave thumbs up to each other and then separate in opposite directions to start the most grueling gun camera dogfight you could ever imagine. Often our wings would pass each other going in opposite directions at relative speeds in excess of 675 miles per hour.

During those spine-tingling training sessions, Tex and I became highly proficient and felt we could whip the world, probably a good attitude for this deadly profession we were about to engage in once assigned to a Pacific Task Force.

On one occasion, I recall turning in on Tex's tail with such a high "G" (gravity) load that Tex's inboard wing stalled, sending him into a vicious spin that seemed to last forever. Miraculously, Tex pulled out extremely close to ground level. This was probably the only flight I ever saw Tex visibly frightened when we returned to base.

On the opposite side of Vero Airport were parked about fifteen aircraft called Brewster Dive-Bombers. This plane was designed specifically for carrier dive-bombing missions. However, the Navy never really experienced any great success with them because of their long cumbersome fuselage and relatively poor takeoff performance from carrier-based operations. To get rid of them, they took out most of the essential instruments and had them translated into Dutch for delivery to the Dutch Navy. It was apparent from the word that got around that the Dutch pilots were concerned about the same poor performance and soon returned those beastly planes to the U.S. Navy, Dutch instruments and all. I figured that's how they ended up parked at the opposite end of Vero Beach Air Station.

Naturally curious, Tex and I went over to these planes and carefully checked them out. We decided to ask the commanding officer if we could run an inspection on a couple of them, that is, to test fly them and then use them for our own enjoyment. With his reluctant okay, we soon had them in shape with the help of a couple of good mechanics. With an instruction manual printed in Dutch and about five hours of sitting in the cockpit learning what all the controls would do, Tex and I were ready to take our first flight. Somehow we decided I would take off first.

After taxiing out to the takeoff spot and sitting there for better than ten minutes, I decided to open the throttle wide and start the roll. After what I considered to be an abnormal length of time going like a bat out of hell down the runway and with serious doubt the plane would ever become airborne, I quickly cut the power and coasted to the end of the runway, coming to a screeching halt just feet from a cyclone fence.

Tex, witnessing this performance, decided to taxi back to the ramp and recheck our power availability. After determining we could easily lift off by cracking the wing flaps, which would give added lift, I gave it another try. This time, with flaps slightly open, this Brewster dive-bombing beast rose smoothly into the air. At that time, this machine reminded me of jumping out of a compact car and attempting to drive a bus. Once airborne, the plane was quite stable, and within a few days, we were attempting a variety of aerobatic maneuvers once it achieved combat speeds up to 170 knots.

Fletcher's Brewster dive bomber over Vero Beach, Florida.

Ensign Wayne "Tex" Collins.

The real adventure came about a week later when Tex and I were just out cruising over the Everglades south of Fort Pierce when, all of a sudden, my cockpit filled up with a large puff of white smoke. Being a very clear day, these weren't clouds I was seeing. I immediately rolled the Plexiglas canopy open and soon learned I had experienced a major oil line break, as a thick stream of pure white smoke poured down the right side of the plane. I radioed to Tex that I had an emergency and he stayed with me for several minutes. I attempted to stretch out a long glide into nearby Vero, but it soon became evident this was swiftly becoming a life or death situation.

Over the radio, I heard Tex yelling, "Get the hell out!"

I had never experienced jumping from a plane before, much less in an emergency situation. After a few short practice grabs for the ripcord, I pulled the beast up into a climb to gain all the altitude I could get and, as the plane slowed down, I grabbed hold of a radar bracket mounted just outside the cockpit and proceeded to climb out. I remembered my training. If you jump, don't hit the tail.

With flames and burning oil streaming down the fuselage, I rolled my body over into a sloppy dive that scared the living crap out of me. Within seconds, I grabbed for my ripcord and — bang! — I felt a quick jerk and began swinging in the air. I made the mistake of not tightening my leg straps before jumping and came rather near to hurting my privates as the parachute snapped open. I experienced a few days of discomfort from severe groin razor burn.

As I descended, I watched this crippled dive-bomber slowly roll over and over before crashing some three miles offshore into the Atlantic Ocean.

As I approached the ground, I maneuvered over to a spot that looked acceptable, and I landed with a heavy splash into the Indian River. A good swimmer, I pulled the life raft from the chute pack and inflated a small dinghy. Working my way over to the riverbed bank, I saw this fully dressed Indian in costume reaching down to give me a hand. Fancy meeting this guy here! He must have thought I was some kind of alien.

Fletcher's advanced fighter training group, Vero Beach. Fletcher is in the back row, second from the left.

Vero Air Base must have learned of my bailout from Tex because I could hear planes overhead starting their routine search procedures. As it turned out, this Seminole Indian had an old Model-T Ford about a quarter of a mile away. But he refused to give me a ride unless I gave him the life raft, which of course I obligingly surrendered for a ride back to civilization.

To end this drama, a Navy search and rescue team picked me up within a few hours. I was committed to an infirmary for a twenty-four hour checkup. Except for my razor burns, all went well. After a day or so, I once again resumed my flying status.

Another unusual event occurred about two weeks later. It began when the Vero Beach commanding officer asked me to fly a Hellcat to Jacksonville Naval Air Station and pick up a new Curtis Helldiver assigned to the Vero Base. As an eager pilot just waiting for new and challenging assignments, I departed for Jacksonville where, upon arrival, someone in Logistics showed me the plane and had me sign a release so I could return to Vero.

As I prepared the simple, brief flight plan, one of the officers asked me if I would be willing to take an ensign waiting to hitch a ride to Miami. Understanding I was only going as far as Vero Beach (roughly halfway to Miami), he elected to be my passenger and fly in the rear gunner slot of the Helldiver. I got the impression he never had any air time in a military combat plane before. After a quick explanation of how his seat's parachute worked, we climbed into the plane for our return trip to Vero.

The control tower alerted me to taxi out to the end of the runway. After completing a routine check of the plane and engine, I received clearance for immediate takeoff. The Curtis Helldiver, although a dive-bomber much like the Brewster dive-bomber, had considerably more power.

I started down the runway with throttle wide open and proceeded to climb out at about 1,000 feet per minute. As I reached 2,000 feet to level off, I pulled back the throttle to reduce power and was startled to find that the hand throttle had become disengaged from the engine and was ineffective. Pushing the throttle full forward also had absolutely no power-controlling effect for regulating aircraft speed with this runaway engine. After convincing myself I should remain calm and above all not let on to my inexperienced ensign passenger that we were in deep trouble, it became apparent the engine was racing wide open, assuring me, at least for the moment, that I wasn't going to experience reduced power that would force an emergency landing. Since my poor ensign passenger had never flown in a dive-bomber, let alone bailing out, I decided I had no choice but to land or crash somewhere on the airfield.

With the Helldiver circling the Jacksonville Naval Air Station at 5,000 feet and the throttle wide open and no way to control power, airspeed soon peaked out at close to 300 miles per hour. It was like sitting in a runaway roller coaster with no way to slow it down.

Under the circumstances, I did the only thing I could do for the moment. Picking up the radio-microphone, I said, "Hello, Jacksonville. Red Fox 32. May Day," which meant I had an emergency. "I have a runaway engine, no throttle control, speed building to maximum limitations, inexperienced passenger riding shotgun. Please advise recommendation."

"Red Fox 32. Jacksonville Control. Stand by." A thirty second pause seemed like a lifetime. "Red Fox 32. Jacksonville Control. Do you have positive flight control except for power adjustment?"

I responded, "Jacksonville Control. Affirmative."

"Red Fox 32. Jacksonville Control. The C.O. advises you to fly down the beach direct to Vero, your home base, and receive further instructions."

By now, a cold sweat was beading across my forehead. Looking in my rearview mirror, I could see my passenger sensed that something might be wrong, but didn't really know what, except that I was sure he knew we were going like a bat out of hell and didn't know why.

"Jacksonville Control. Red Fox 32. Will comply with your instructions to return to Vero. Please alert Operations to pull out their crash crew, fire trucks, and anything else. I have no idea just how, short of running out of gas, I will get this crippled bomber back to earth in one piece."

Vero was approximately 190 miles away due south.

With that, I headed speedily down the Florida east coast to Vero Beach Naval Air Station about forty minutes away. But at that uncontrollable speed I might have arrived even sooner. Thank God the weather was clear with sunny skies. Keeping a keen eye on the engine gauges, I wondered just how long this monster would fly with full power before the engine blew apart. The situation reminded me of a guy running a marathon with extremely high blood pressure.

About fifteen minutes out from Vero, I radioed in.

"Vero Control. Red Fox 32. Do your receive me?"

"Red Fox 32, we hear you. What is your flight condition?"

"Vero Control. My flight controls are okay except this plane has no throttle control, and airspeed is maximum with a runaway engine. By the way, I have another problem. Also carrying an inexperienced passenger who's as nervous as a dog shitting razor blades."

"Red Fox 32, we have you in sight, Emergency crews standing by. Circle Vero at present altitude. Will advise."

Two minutes pass.

"Red Fox 32. Vero Control. We will give you an option. Take it five miles out to sea and bail out, or attempt a landing by making a dead-stick landing (killing the engine) or making a semi-controlled power approach by using the mixture control as a throttle."

"Vero Control. Red Fox 32. Can't bail out with inexperienced passenger. Will elect to land with mixture control. Will circle for thirty minutes practicing the effects of a mixture control power regulation."

"Red Fox 32. We will await your results. Good luck."

For a few short moments, I recalled my training at Olathe where I learned to hit seven landings in the small circle. From where I was coming from, this sounded like a good idea. I knew if I could fully retard the mixture control slowly, that would

Fletcher and his "Hellcat."

gradually shut down with reasonable power control. Advancing the mixture, a surge of power would be experienced.

It also occurred to me that if I missed the runway, it would be all over.

After several high-speed trips around Vero, as if I were in the Daytona 500, it became apparent that using the mixture control as an emergency throttle was a pretty good idea. But first I had to kill this high speed before a landing could be accomplished. After all, there was a big difference from 300 mph to a safe landing speed of 85 to 90 mph.

"Vero Control. Red Fox 32. Ready to attempt a mixture control landing. Will start steep climb to reduce air speed, then start a wide five-mile approach pattern."

As the climb pushed upward, the speed diminished rapidly. When it hit 125 knots, I dropped the wheels and flaps and shut down the mixture to reduce power.

"Vero Control. Red Fox 32. Two miles out. Air speed 120. Looking good."

I began to realize that I probably would have only one shot at landing. To attempt a power-on again wave-off at this point of the landing could be fatal.

As the end of the runway rapidly approached, I could only reduce the airspeed to about 115 knots (about 132 mph), retarding the mixture control without killing the engine. I just knew I needed the full length of the runway.

Anticipating I would glide over the end of the runway, I slammed the mixture shut, killing the engine. Seconds later, the wheels screeched on the hot pavement, well above the recommended normal landing speed. With a sigh of relief, I jockeyed the brakes in spurts, burning rubber like a Daytona 500 racing car on the corner turns. Coasting breathlessly to the end of the runway with a cyclone fence coming up fast in front of me, I pressed the left rudder pedal into the floor to cause a mild ground loop just a few yards from the steel-wire fence. Within seconds, ambulances, fire trucks, and rescue crews were swarming around my plane.

Fletcher pilots a Brewster Dive Bomber.

The plane did not crash into the fence. I couldn't believe it. Jumping out, I walked over to my passenger, and asked him how he was doing under the circumstances. God, was he thankful to be down. Over and over he thanked me for getting him down safely. Except for sparing him the risky experience of bailing out at sea, believe me, it was my own ass I was really concerned about.

After a few minutes, a mechanic peeled off the engine cowling to examine the throttle. He found that some mechanic had left out a cotter pin that caused the throttle rod and carburetor gas control to separate. That meant that no matter where I moved the throttle, there would be no connected reaction on the carburetor gas control. Fortunately, the carburetor was designed to snap into the wide open throttle position under such circumstances, causing the engine to race at full power.

After an emergency briefing and a physical, which was always mandatory following a trauma such as this, I was released for a few days to rest to make a full recovery.

Before leaving this advanced flight training base, one last episode occurred that tested my ability and imagination.

It was a clear afternoon just days after experiencing my wild ride from Jacksonville with a disconnected throttle. This time, as I was approaching Vero Beach and requested landing instructions, another chilling emergency was about to take place.

After being cleared for landing by Vero Tower Control, I started going over the landing checklist of my assigned personal Brewster dive-bomber. Reaching over, I engaged the down lever for the wheels. The visual indicator showed that the left wheel went into a locked down position, but the right wheel did not go down.

The Tower, which was observing my landing approach, barked out over the mike, "Red Fox 32. Take a wave-off . . . I say, take a wave-off. Your right wheel did not disengage."

"Roger, Vero Tower," I replied. "I see that my indicator is telling me the same thing."

Instinctively, I immediately advanced power climbing back to the landing holding pattern. After reaching the prescribed

Curtiss SB2C Helldiver.

altitude of 1,000 feet. I circled Vero and reached down to retract my right wheel, the only gear down and locked, but, lo and behold, it refused to retract. This left me with a very unusual situation, forcing me to make a critical one-wheel landing. If I were not careful, the aircraft could cartwheel end over end and perhaps even cause a fire if fuel broke loose. It had seemed like only yesterday that I had faced a full throttle disconnect in a Curtis Helldiver. Now this situation required every bit of flying talent I possessed. This time, however, I was not confronted with an onboard passenger. Whatever happened involved my ass only.

Circling the field tower control, I discussed various options. After several times trying to raise or lower wheels, it became apparent that the left wheel was going to remain locked down and the right wheel was going to remain locked up.

Still circling Vero, I received my few options to this unsolvable situation.

Finally I blurted out: "Vero Tower Control. Red Fox 32. Let me suggest what I think is best."

"Please express your opinion, Red Fox 32. Go ahead. We have the Chief of Maintenance standing by. All fire crews are in place on the runway. Give us your thoughts."

"Vero Tower. Red Fox 32. It would be the best and safest for me to exhaust all fuel before a landing attempt. If things don't go smoothly during the landing, then at least fire will be minimized."

"Red Fox 32. Good thinking. Continue to orbit Vero and keep us advised."

"Vero Tower. Roger. Will advise."

Roughly an hour and forty-five minutes went by, bringing reserve fuel down to only a few gallons in the main tank. Three or four final efforts to disengage the locked up wheel failed. Now the moment of truth was at hand.

Hanging in close to the field boundary to ensure reaching a runway, I decided to begin a final emergency approach. As I started down, I said to myself, "Tighten all your safety straps and land at a higher than normal speed so it will be possible to fly the right wing into the runway, rather than stalling the wing and having it slam into the ground."

Mentally, this approach sounded reasonable because it would be more likely than not that the aircraft would veer off to the right as the right wing dragged on the ground. On the other hand, by allowing the wing to stall and slam into the ground, there would be a good chance of losing directional control and maybe even cartwheel, leading to total aircraft destruction.

As I approached the runway at 120 knots, the left wheel was about to touch the runway and roll. At 110 knots, I actually was able to fly with the right wing up and the left wheel on the runway. This allowed me to maintain directional control with the rudder because of my excessive speed.

Ever so slowly I flew the right wing onto the runway as smoothly as I could. As it started to drag against the asphalt, the propeller began to bend blades. I was still moving down the runway, sliding straight on my right wing tip: 80 knots . . . 60 knots . . . 30 knots. . . . The plane was drifting right because of the right wing dragging. Sparks were flying everywhere from the prop and from the right wing tip. Fifteen knots — all power was off, but the plane slid only fifteen feet off the designated runway.

Within seconds, the plane came to a screeching halt. I instantly looked around. There was no fire. The experience was a complete success. In a flashing moment, I recalled how important it was to hit that small circle without power when I was trained in Kansas, as if my instructor just knew one day I would be faced with such an emergency.

I unleashed my safety straps and was out of there in seconds. Immediately, the fire and maintenance crews took over. A rapid review of the wing and propeller revealed relatively little damage.

Just about three weeks to the day, the prop had been replaced, the wing and flap had been repaired, and the plane was ready for its first test flight after that impromptu one-wheel landing.

As for me, I had had enough thrills in my final days at Vero to last a lifetime. Deep inside, I was ready to leave for my first combat squadron assignment in the Pacific.

Soon this phase of advanced fighter training came to an end, and I realized the next stop would be a new assignment with the Pacific fleet. Just where or with what squadron produced a hidden anxiety that lasted a few fleeting days before Washington would cut the new orders for assignment. As it turned out, my good friend, Tex Collins, received orders to a new squadron, which was different from mine. I hated to part company with Tex because we had learned so much together during our mock dogfight training.

After receiving my orders to join Fighting Squadron Eight in San Diego, California, it began to sink in that combat was not that far off. I was almost ready to go to war.

Arriving in San Diego a short time after leaving Vero, I checked in with the squadron commander and hastily became acquainted with Fighting Eight's combat history. Soon it was routine combat training again, but this time more seriously, knowing well that we would be meeting our Japanese enemy just as soon as a carrier would become available in San Francisco.

For the next six weeks, we flew our planes up to the Watsonville Naval Air Station just out of Carmel, off Monterey Bay. Here we practiced day and night strikes shooting rockets into tow targets. These were wooden platforms, or sleds, that were towed by a destroyer out in Monterey Bay. Every day it was ten to twelve hours of practice dogfights, smoke-bombing the sleds, and a variety of special combat events.

The squadron maintained detailed and accurate records on our sharpshooting. Much to my surprise, I led the squadron of forty-eight pilots with the highest scores in vertical dive rocket bombing and was in the upper 7 percent hitting a towed flying sleeve with 50 caliber bullets making 180 degree vertical dive overhead runs. This was achieved by starting out several thousand feet above and forward of the tow plane. Turning back to intercept the tow plane, the attack started by rolling upside down and diving straight down at the sleeve while it was passing beneath you. While passing through the vertical in a dive, we would start firing 50 caliber bullets with their nose colored with paint to identify hits into the sleeve after returning to base. God, this was exciting!

F6F Grumman Hellcats on air patrol over Guam.

Sometimes dive speeds would approach 400 knots as we would start to fire our guns. Heading the list in scoring was equivalent to being the top gun in today's Navy. Honestly, at that level of training, I considered all of us top guns, some being just slightly more proficient than others, but all super pilots who each in his own right was the Navy's cream of the crop.

It doesn't get any better than that.

While at Watsonville Air Station, daily briefings were given on the status of our carrier action presently heavily engaged in the air battles decisive in establishing advanced air bases for our planned long-range bomber assault directly on the Japanese homeland. During this period reports came in to accelerate our advanced training to replace Air Groups being hammered daily. American airmen were reported outnumbered three to one, and with casualties running high it became apparent our squadron would be welcomed to help balance the air power. The naval campaign to capture Okinawa also took heavy casualties.

It was during this time that the USS Franklin, another of our large Essex-class aircraft carriers, was hit by a kamikaze just off the coast of Kyushu and began burning fiercely. The Franklin was hit only minutes before it was scheduled to start an air assault. The deck was loaded with planes full of rockets and ammunition that later, as the fire spread, resulted in a Fourth of July spectacular display. Ammunition and 5-inch rockets were going off in all directions, causing considerable damage to the ship's superstructure and its own Air Group planes. The Franklin was so badly damaged that the skipper's first reaction was to abandon ship to help save the crew. Deciding to hold her ground, the crew desperately fought on to keep her afloat. Had the skipper given the signal to abandon ship, it would have been a devastating psychological victory for the Japanese and a major blow to the Franklin's crew. With courage and dignity at the height of the battle, the crew got the ship to maintain a limp but floating condition long enough to withdraw. With the help of a naval "Iron Curtain" around the Franklin and air support from the rest of the task force, the

Franklin steamed out of the combat zone while crews extinguished the flames and she was taken in tow.

As the task force inflicted heavy destruction on the Japanese strongholds, the Japanese kamikazes struck back, causing severe damage to several of our ships. Despite the losses, this seemed to be a turning point in the war. Japanese aircraft and ships took heavy casualties during a period when conventional warfare by the Japanese had virtually ceased. It appeared almost everything was now suicidal as the kamikazes made their last ditch stand to break through our aerial defenses.

8

Entering the
Pacific War

Shortly after our Thanksgiving holiday in 1944, word came in to the Air Group Commander that our aircraft carrier was due to arrive in San Francisco Bay. There, our squadron boarded the ship destined for Pearl Harbor, Maui, then on to the South Pacific war zone.

Two days before boarding the carrier, we took off one last time for a little aerial sport called "tail chasing." After climbing up to about 12,000 feet, our six planes would fly within ten feet of each other's tail and then, upon a signal from our leader, we would begin a series of complex aerobatic maneuvers in a "follow-the-leader" formation requiring a high level of flying skill and concentration to avoid an in-flight collision. This sport was similar to the demonstrations of the renowned "Blue Angels," the Navy's crack aerobatic formation team. After about twenty minutes of this highly dangerous aerial sport, we were just about ready to head back to the Alameda Naval Air Base (just off the Golden Gate Bridge), when "Lumgutz" (strictly a nickname) Lamoreaux, a seasoned veteran from an earlier combat tour, called out on the intercom, "This is Hellcat Leader Seven. Follow me." Being our leader, that is exactly what we were trained to do.

Again, closing up in tight tail formation, "Lumgutz" decided to roll over and dive toward the Golden Gate Bridge. I thought that once he was within a couple of thousand feet of the bridge, he would signal us to pull up to pass safely over the bridge. Hell, no! I should have known. This crazy bastard continued to head straight down at the bridge, levels out fifty feet above the water, and aims straight at the underside of the bridge. Within seconds, I realized this was it. We were going to go under this tremendous span! One by one, the four of us passed under the bridge flying like a bat out of hell, then pulling straight up to 10,000 feet to join up in vee formation.

Within two minutes after joining up, a white Hellcat pulled up along side of us, piloted by a U.S. Marine. His plane had "POLICE" printed on the tail under the Navy blue star. There was no doubt in our minds. We were in serious trouble. A moment later, over our intercom radio, a blast came across, "Commander in Charge. You are under arrest. Report immediately to the Alameda Naval Air Station."

Scared and overflowing with anxiety, we taxied, one by one, up to the parking ramp. As the engines were cut, each of our planes was met by a Marine Military Police Officer, who immediately handcuffed us and hauled us off to the nearest brig. I guessed that had there not been a serious Pacific conflict going on at this time, our asses would have been cooked.

The following day, we heard a Captain's hearing was scheduled. Under guard, we were escorted by a Marine Police Patrol to the hearing that was to determine our fate. After entering the base headquarters, we were led into a room facing a table lined with our senior officers, one of whom was our squadron commander. There, Lumgutz claimed responsibility for the rest of us and took a severe reprimand. He was fined $2,000 and the rest of us were fined $800, which was a lot of money at that time when the average weekly paycheck was $50. We were all placed on probation after boarding our carrier. This continued until we reached Pearl Harbor. For a short while, we were referred to as the "gutsy four," those brave warriors experiencing the rare thrill of breezing under the Golden Gate. With the Pacific War now in full swing, this incident was quickly forgotten. Except for the $800 I was fined, the experience was a good memory that will stay with me the rest of my life. As I look back now, Lumgutz was a seasoned vet. He already had just about every medal the Navy had to offer. There was no question the Navy needed him badly in the Pacific again.

Three days out of San Francisco, I began to experience that queasy feeling of seasickness. Until you develop sea legs, you spend a good bit of time looking down the hole of a commode. After about a week, however, this sickness slowly subsides. Then you get the feeling you are a full-fledged seaman.

As the sun broke over the horizon one morning, we experienced our first glimpse of old Diamond Head glistening just off the coast of Oahu. Diamond Head is a sight to behold and lives up to its reputation as Oahu's most talked about landmark. The following day, our assigned carrier, the USS Long Island steamed into Pearl Harbor. There, for the first time, we saw up close the shocking devastation the attack on Pearl Harbor had on our Pacific fleet.

By the time we anchored in Pearl Harbor, things were running in high gear. Ships of all shapes and sizes were coming in and out of Pearl with armaments and supplies for our fleet. During our trip by sea from San Francisco to Pearl, we were inundated with serious lectures covering the most recent data obtained from Intelligence about the "Japs." We discussed our most likely combat strike locations – and we learned their habits, their aeronautical strengths and, most of all, their weaknesses. Finally, the so-called Intelligence experts gave us advice on the art of dogfighting tactics and evasive action concepts, including just about anything that would help us to stay alive in the heat of battle.

Shortly after arriving at Pearl, we quickly found our way over to the Royal Hawaiian Hotel, one of Waikiki's beach hot spots at the time. By 1944, the Navy seemed to have taken over operational control of the hotel for the purpose of using it as an emergency hospital, with the bars and dance floors swinging most of the night for the military's enjoyment.

The following day, all members of Air Group Eight were ordered back to the carrier USS Long Island only to learn our orders were to pick up our individually assigned fighters (Hellcats) and

Squadron humor; while temporarily on Saipan.

head down to Maui. Once there, we were to await further assignment back to the USS Rudyerd Bay aircraft carrier, which was in for major overhaul resulting from typhoon damage.

Soon the squadron departed Pearl in our new Hellcats, flying in groups of four, heading down the chain of islands, past Molokai where lepers were sheltered. As we approached the Island of Maui from about 11,000 feet, the first thing that impressed me was the twin volcanoes, which were just about at my altitude level.

Starting our approach around the large crater, we dropped our wheels and landed at the Maui Naval Air Station in Hawaii where we had our B.O.Q. (bachelor officer's quarters) assignment for the next twenty-five or so days. We knew we were in for some comprehensive group training. As the combat zone became ever so near, each of us took on a more serious attitude about improving our flying abilities. For the next several days, it was up at five in the morning, a briefing at 6:30, followed by a heavy schedule of simulated dogfights, dive-bombing, rocket launch firing, and practice carrier landings.

It was during this period shortly after arriving at Maui that our Air Group Commander ordered our fighter and torpedo bombers out to sea to intercept the USS Antietam that was cruising about 140 miles offshore. This event was intended to provide each of us with several carrier landings which, while necessary, was perhaps the most stressful flying experience.

Returning to Maui after a short stay aboard the USS Antietam, our planes flew out to sea about 100 miles and boarded the Saratoga around 6:30 p.m. Following a brief meeting, our planes, one by one, were catapulted into a nearly jet-black sky. Flying above a carrier task force after dark was a tricky task, simply because the ships could not have lights for fear of attracting enemy submarines. However, the destroyers acting as escorts and the carriers were permitted to have a cone light, which could only be seen from the air for identification.

As our planes gathered information, the pilots would peel off one by one and enter a landing pattern around the carrier. For

Fighting Squadron Eight emblem.

Lt. William "Lumgutz" Lamoreaux, leader of
Fighting Squadron Eight.

me, this was my first night landing ever. What an unforgettable moment.

During the third night of this operation, fighter pilot Willie Williams snapped his "arresting hook" that stops the plane when landing on the carrier deck. Willie's Hellcat continued down the flight deck, plowing through the emergency barriers and then going over the side of the ship, crashing into the sea. Although Willie lost his flashlight escaping from the plane, he was lucky to signal the ship's rear guard destroyer with a whistle hanging from his life vest. Within minutes, Willie was thrown a rescue line. He managed to climb aboard the rolling escort destroyer in a frighteningly rough sea. That was the same night I found it almost impossible to identify the Saratoga from the other ships in the Task Force. The cone lights did not reflect their true colors for positive identification due to a hazy condition. As I started my landing approach toward the ship I thought was the Saratoga, I failed to see our landing signal officer holding the familiar fluorescent paddles to guide pilots into a safe landing position. Not seeing the signal officer, I was forced to take a "wave-off" and go around for another try. For the next five passes, I faced the same situation. When it came time to land, there was no visible signal officer to give me the final landing cut in this jet-black sky.

As I made my sixth pass and approached the stern of the ship, the ship's skipper released a blast of light from one of his searchlights. I was surprised to see the outline of our lead destroyer beneath me. Scared to death, I suddenly realized why there was no signal officer to guide me down. As I had done for the five previous passes, I opened the throttle and started rapidly to climb out and away from the destroyer. Recognizing the Saratoga was the ship directly behind the lead destroyer, a new seventh pass was the way to go. This time, as I flew up the rear, lining up with the ship's fluorescent wake, the signal officer finally became clearly visible. As I approached the ship's stern, the signal officer pulled his fluorescent paddle across his chest, the signal I needed to cut my power. With a thud and a jerk I had landed safely. What a relief! My heart was racing faster than the

Hellcat's propeller. After successfully boarding the Saratoga, the captain of the lead destroyer sent a message over to our carrier, suggesting they nickname me "Flush Deck" – the reason being the destroyer I attempted to land on was a Fletcher Class destroyer named after Admiral Fletcher (no relation that I'm aware of). This destroyer was identified by its unbroken deck-line from stem to stern. Had I crash-landed on the destroyer, it would have had a "flush deck." So the nickname stuck with me for the rest of my Pacific tour of duty.

After completing several successful night carrier landings on the Saratoga, I would discover that the worst was yet to come.

By the end of the week, our night landing exercises aboard the USS Saratoga came to an end. Gathering in the ready room for a final briefing, we learned that we were two planes short because of Willie's crash landing into the sea and Floyd Miles's crash into the bridge superstructure, which totally disabled his plane. Commander Paul Duke asked for three volunteers to fly back to our land base in the belly of a torpedo bomber. Always ready to accommodate the skipper, I accepted the challenge to ride back to Maui with Commander Cagle, the skipper of Torpedo Squadron Eight. Joining us in the torpedo bomber ride were Ensigns Robert Burke and Robert Einer. When the three of us gathered on the Saratoga's flight deck to return to Maui, we had to decide who would ride up in the rear gunner's bubble and who would ride in the belly of the bomber. We agreed to flip a coin. The first toss I won the gunner bubble seat from Burke. Then I flipped the coin again and won the gunner's seat from Einer. With Lady Luck still with me, I climbed into the torpedo bomber first so I could crawl up into the rear-facing bubble gunner's seat. From that vantage point, I could see everything above the plane. Following me, Burke and Einer climbed into their forward-facing seats looking directly at my legs dangling in their eyes from my perch in the gunner's bubble. The only visibility Burke and Einer had was from a small window in the door of the plane's belly.

After we were all settled into our places, Commander Cagle taxied onto the catapult and within minutes we were shot off the

Aboard the USS Saratoga, 1945.

bow of the Saratoga and were airborne. Looking rearward through my gunner's glass bubble vantage point, I enjoyed a tremendous view of the Saratoga, which we left behind for our return trip to Maui. Sitting in the bubble, I realized this trip was the only time I ever flew with the squadron as a passenger and not as the pilot of the plane.

As we began our departing climb into beautiful clear blue sky, two other torpedo bombers joined us on our wing. It was only about thirty-five minutes into our return flight when Commander Cagle radioed back to us on the intercom that he was experiencing engine trouble. I noticed something was wrong by the interrupted sound of our humming engine. About ten minutes went by when the commander radioed back again to tell us to prepare for a water landing. Immediately, all three of us snugged up our safety harness, preparing for an inevitable crash water landing. As the plane gradually approached the rippling sea, Burke and Einer reached out their arms to support themselves against my dangling legs. As we neared the rough sea, I found myself starting to panic because I had never experienced knocking out the small emergency escape window in the plastic bubble. As I tried to unlatch the emergency escape window, I found it impossible to open the latch. The plane was now fifty feet from the ocean when I took a frantic swing with my elbow, causing the bubble escape window to fly out. Within seconds, the plane was skipping along the top of the waves when I heard a violent crack near the bottom of the plane as it came swiftly to rest on the ocean's surface.

Without hesitation, I quickly squeezed my body through the small emergency opening and grabbed on to one of the machine gun barrels for support. Once safely out of the plane, I jumped over to the other side of the bomber where the rear door was located to see if I could assist Burke and Einer still in the plane's belly. As I pulled open the door and peered into the belly of the plane, I knew we had problems: the bottom of the floor was half-filled with a pool of bloody water. Underneath was a big gaping hole torn in the plane's belly, which is what I probably heard when we hit the water. For several minutes, I tried frantically to find my fellow airmen. I was unaware that Commander Cagle had managed to climb out and inflate a four-man emergency raft, which started drifting away from the downed plane in the high winds.

As I continued my search in the belly of the plane for Burke and Einer, Commander Cagle was screaming his lungs out telling me to clear the plane before it sinks. As I looked rearward, there, about 500 yards behind the crash point, were two inflated parachutes that obviously opened on impact. It appeared that both Burke and Einer were sucked out of the plane by the rushing water that cracked open the plane's belly when the plane crashed into the sea. Realizing there was nothing more I could do to save them, I turned my attention to Commander Cagle and the emergency raft. Suddenly, I recalled the water filling the bomber and their hands sliding down my dangling legs when the plane hit the sea. By this time, I was faced with trying to catch up with the commander's inflated raft. Swimming desperately for more than fifteen minutes, I was able to grab a line hanging from the raft. With the help of Cagle, I pulled myself aboard and fell inside the raft, completely exhausted. It was less than a half-hour when a rescue ship, responding to the commander's "Mayday" call for help, came into view and took us both aboard for our unscheduled trip back to Maui.

Several days later, Commander Cagle presented me with a "Letter of Commendation" for what he considered was a gallant effort to save my two comrades.

I often think about that coin-tossing event back on the deck of the Saratoga. By a sheer stroke of luck that determined life or death for me in the torpedo bomber, I continued my almost mystical quest for survival.

About this same period, our U.S. Marines were securing Guam. It was one of the early battles of the Mariana Islands. By the time Fighting Squadron Eight arrived, the island was fast becoming a major depot for accumulating vast amounts of strategic war materials to assault the Mariana chain of islands, which included Rota, Tinian, and Saipan. It was at the latter islands

The Sacred Heart of Jesus

Photograph of actual medal worn by Lt. Comdr.
Charles J. Fletcher during three separate navy airplane crashes.
Later worn by son Jeffrey during a twin engine emergency
landing resulting in a crash. From 1942 through 1999,
this medal was lost two times for a period in excess of 11 months
then found outdoors on the premises. This medal now is in
the possession of son Jeffrey. In 1945, in the South Pacific,
this medal survived three days and four hours after an
emergency landing. The history of this medal is considered
miraculous.

where fierce ground and air battles were fought at the expense of thousands of Marines and several airmen all of whom operated from a large task group of aircraft carriers. After arriving in the waters off Guam, Air Group Eight flew missions throughout the chain of Marianas. Finally with the successful assault on Saipan completed, the Seabees moved their heavy construction equipment ashore to rebuild the heavily bombarded airstrip at Kagman Field. With the airstrip completed, our squadron was ordered ashore. There, several Quonset huts were constructed to provide us with housing during our brief stay on the island. We lived on this devastated island over the next several weeks, an island that became the second major depot for receiving huge amounts of war materials. Just a few miles off the coast of Saipan the small island of Tinian became the home base for the famous B-29 bombers. From the Tinian vantage point the B-29s could now fly directly to the Philippines and on to the mainland of Japan.

While our squadron was assigned ashore on Saipan, Japanese were still holding out back in the rocky cliffs. On occasion, we would form a small group of three or four and wander off into the nearby hills just looking for excitement. During these short trips, we found many bodies (mostly believed to be Japanese soldiers) just inside the caves. As I look back now, we were just plain foolish because word often came back to camp reporting sightings of Japanese soldiers still in hiding.

I will never forget entering one cave, which was obviously used to house wounded Japanese. There we found six skeletons still lying in beds. On the front of their hospital bunks were charts of their conditions. Several graphs showed a red line signaling a sharp decline, perhaps indicating death.

Except for daily patrols off Saipan, our squadron was able to borrow an Army carryall Jeep to visit Saipan Harbor, which was used for arriving and departing U.S. ships. Two miles from the entry zone, we located hundreds of skeletons lying on the beach just where they had met their fatal bullet. By the time we got there, insects had devoured their flesh completely. It was apparent there had been just too many bodies to bury.

Walking along the stretch of this beach, it became an obsession to try to match the various jawbones with the skulls that for whatever reason had become detached. By this time, we were hardened to death and lacked any concern for their lives or family history. This beach was the final resting place for hundreds of bodies, a sickening site that has embedded itself into my memory to this very day. Despite this hellish horror, a few of our hardened pilots would actually select a few of the skulls stripped of their flesh. After accumulating several skulls, they would string them onto a rope and hang them from the entry of their Quonset huts.

Just a few miles away over in the bay area where all of the activity on Saipan was taking place, I experienced my first real drunk. There were several Quonset huts joined end to end, which were used for relaxation. This had to be the longest bar I had ever seen! One day while in the area, we visited this bar. First we had to check in with the sentry and to surrender all our knives and holstered guns at the door. They didn't want any drunken bastards starting a shooting war, which I understood did happen before our arrival on the island.

This was one of those occasions. A few of our boys were there one afternoon, drinking and bullshitting the afternoon away. The best booze in the house was only ten cents per drink, and let me tell you, a single drink was no less than three ounces. After a couple of hours, I knew I had consumed too much. I felt completely intoxicated, stone drunk was more like it. The last thing I remembered was being pulled by the arms back to a U.S. Army Jeep equipped with a canopy over two wooden seats on each side of the vehicle. They dragged my limp body onto the floor of the Jeep. At that time, I can tell you I felt no pain.

On the way back to our quarters at Kagman Field, I was later told two of these guys started a fight over my immobile body. In the process, they must have kicked the hell out of my ribs and trampled my head. When I became conscious the following noon, I thought I had died a thousand deaths. I was so sick that I remained bedridden for two more days.

Not being able to explain the circumstances, it was apparent my skipper was nothing less than pissed off. As I slowly overcame the effects of alcohol toxicity, I found myself nursing a shiner over my right eye and body bruises on my legs and hips, caused by the brawl in the jeep. To this day, I have not allowed myself to experience a drunken condition like that again.

On one occasion we flew our Hellcats up to the end of Saipan to a place called Marpi Point. This was the site of a short airstrip on the edge of a cliff used occasionally for bringing fresh supplies to Marines. Marpi Point was where the Marines overran the Japanese at the edge of the cliff. Many jumped to their deaths rather than be taken prisoner. At the bottom of the cliff, the soldiers' skeletons lay exactly where they had landed.

At times, war is madness. Marpi Point was one of those times. Several Marines and Navy personnel searched for these skulls for the purpose of recovering the gold in their teeth. Some of the guys had a satchel full of gold fillings. It seemed the Japanese only used gold to repair their teeth.

Soon, the skipper received word that we were ready to board the carrier USS Bennington. After leaving Saipan, our task force cruised down to a small island in the South Pacific called Eniwetok. There, the carrier refueled and gathered supplies. This was the final prelude for the invasion of Japan's mainland.

Often we would see the B-29s out of Tinian returning from their bombing missions on Iwo Jima. On many occasions our mission was to intercept the 29s and escort them partway back. More often than not we would spot a B-29 that had received shrapnel damage that threatened its safe return to the Tinian base.

During one of my sorties that took our air group some 260 miles from our carrier to intercept several reported Japanese munition ships, my life, in one brief moment, changed forever. During one of my passes I heard a thud. Simultaneously, I felt a sharp jolt just forward of the cockpit in the Hellcat's engine section. Not sure just what had happened, I joined in formation with my squadron for our return to the USS Bennington. Over the next

Lt. Commander Charles Fletcher, over Saipan.

thirty minutes, I sensed a gradual power reduction so much so that I knew an emergency water landing was inevitable.

Quickly I calculated my position as being slightly less than halfway back to the carrier. As my mind raced like a calculator, I decided to attempt a water landing as opposed to bailing out. Since the seas were relatively calm, I decided to set the Hellcat down parallel in the trough of two swells. Approaching the water at about twenty-five feet, airspeed 85 knots, I grabbed the Sacred Heart Medal around my neck. This religious medal was given to me by my Aunt Natalie Mosner (my mother's sister) just before departing for the service. I could hear her say as the water came up to my plane, "If you ever have an occasion when you sense real danger, just grab this Sacred Heart Medal and you will overcome your fears." That's exactly what I did as the plane splashed through the trough of the two parallel waves. The plane settled in with a relatively short stop. My shoulder harness held me firmly in the seat. Within minutes I was able to crawl out into the water and inflate my one-man raft. Before I was able to clear myself fifty feet away, the plane tail pitched up as the weight of the engine began to send the plane to a watery grave.

As I bobbed around in what became fairly rough seas, three other members of my squadron buzzed my position, which gave me courage and hope that I would soon be rescued. Because it was around noon when I went down and I was still over 100 miles from the USS Bennington, I had little hope I would be rescued before nightfall.

As it turned out, I continued to float uncontrollably for more than two days (actually 52-and-a-half hours in all), riding six-to-eight foot swells like a roller coaster during daylight hours, hoping to spot anything on the horizon. In the evening, the sea was calmer, and I could catch a few winks now and then, which was difficult because of the salt water sloshing around the bottom of my little raft. I really didn't want to fall asleep as I was afraid of missing something, anything, appearing anywhere around me that could be picked up in the moonlight.

I rigged up a rain-catching canvas from part of my life jacket, but it didn't rain.To protect myself from the scorching sun during the day, I wore my pilot's helmet. I removed my shoes because of swollen feet but left on my soaking wet socks that protected my sore feet from the blazing rays of the sun.

Looking down at my dear Sacred Heart Medal, I noticed the salt water caused the dye in the red heart to bleed through the medal's plastic case. I placed the medal on the edge of the raft while I stared at it for hours, praying. I never stopped praying. I kept Aunt Nat's precious medal from falling off the raft by tying its chain with something that was connected to my jacket. This medal, though faded from the aqueous Pacific environment, is still in my son's possession this day.

After the second day, two sharks appeared and began a ritual pattern of circling me in an unusual movement of two turns left, then two turns right. I was afraid they would try to attack my life raft. On one occasion, one of the sharks broke its routine and cut across in front of the raft and rolled its white belly up at me.

My survival kit included a can of fresh water, two candy Charms, a fishing line with a hook on it, and two flares. The Charms and all but two ounces of water were gone after two days struggling to stay awake so I wouldn't miss a passing ship on the horizon. I began to feel the effects of no food and only a sip of water left, which I tried to stretch out as long as I could. I dropped the fish line over the side of the raft. That proved to be a futile exercise. I didn't get as much as a bite. A fisherman I wasn't. As for rain, the sky could not have been more clear and beautiful.

On the third day at about 3 o'clock in the afternoon, I spotted what appeared to be dark smoke on the horizon. After rising to the top of several swells, I began seeing the outline of what I thought was a ship. Having two yellow smoke emergency flares in my life vest, I immediately released one. Within seconds, a tall column of dense yellow smoke started to rise. This was the standard emergency signal used by our downed airmen. As I continued to rise and fall in the heavy swells, it soon became apparent that this was a ship, and they evidently had seen my emergency flares. I prayed to God that this wasn't the enemy. I just had to wait it out. At this point I couldn't have cared less.

To be sure they saw me, I released my second flare of yellow dense smoke. Within minutes, I could see the ship gliding into position for my rescue. At last, there appeared a whaleboat from the ship with several seamen aboard. As it approached, it was obvious that these guys had beards so I was certain they were not Japanese seamen. All Japanese I had seen were beardless.

They approached with caution through the rough seas. When they felt conditions were safe, they threw a life preserver at me with a rope attached. Clutching the life preserver, I counted the seconds as they slowly towed me in close to their boat where they could lift me aboard with their hands. Boy, were these guys excited to be part of this rescue! But I was the one most grateful! It was around 4:30 in the afternoon. The Sacred Heart, I truly believed, saved my life. It was not my time to go.

Once aboard the ship, I learned that the name of the vessel was the Christy Mathewson, a liberty ship that was delivering supplies to a port in the Philippines. The captain, after snapping several photos, had his crew carry me down to his quarters where we exchanged a wide range of information. During this processing, the captain told me just how lucky I was. He said the only reason he came in contact with my downed position was that he received instructions to deviate from his course twenty miles south of his charted position because of an enemy submarine sighting. By doing so, he came in sight of my emergency flare.

For the next several days, I enjoyed the cruise while the captain attempted to return me to my carrier. That was not easy, however, as I needed to transfer to a submarine for further transportation to a point of interception with a PT boat. Boarding that sub scared the hell out of me. Being cooped up under the sea just wasn't for me. Several days later, the sub came up and surfaced, and I was transferred to a U.S. PT boat, better known as a Patrol Torpedo boat. Within minutes I waved goodbye to the sub crew and sped swiftly off. Days later I rejoined my squadron and a brief party was held. All were happy to see my return.

During the days that followed, our daily routine involved strenuous physical conditioning, combat tactics lectures, and numerous aerial reconnaissance sorties just to maintain our aerial security. Soon, after heading deep within the combat zone, we began to make our daily low-level flights around the task force just to ensure no surprises lay ahead. After a morning briefing, we learned the task force's next mission would play the final role in bringing this ugly conflict to an end. Although we didn't know for sure, our instincts told us we were rapidly approaching the mainland of Japan. Word soon filtered down that the task force was now about 550 miles or so from the Japanese mainland.

It was only natural to feel the tension. Most of us were just itching for a good fight if only to dissipate the adrenaline that was rushing through our veins.

Each day thereafter, we would be in the air for daily patrols, continuing our escort for the B-29s assigned to attack Iwo Jima, the Philippines, and the other last remaining strongholds of the Japanese. With each new daily briefing, it became clear that our next critical raids would involve the Japanese mainland. We all knew this effort would culminate months of planning by Intelligence. There was no doubt in our minds that this was intended to be the final battle of the Pacific War.

Everyone in my squadron believed most of the hotshot Japanese fighter pilots were expended by this time, only because the kamikaze suicide pilots were Japan's last resort to defend the skies over the mainland. There were fewer and fewer reports of aerial opposition. There was little doubt the rising sun was about to set.

Of course, there was always the risk that Japanese aircraft were still able to throw one more curve to defend their Japanese honor. Thus, we continued to maintain a serious attitude, coupled with daily briefings that detailed just how to survive should we get shot down. I had already become a seasoned veteran.

There were rumors that the Japanese would cut our throats from ear to ear and allow us to bleed to death slowly. Intelligence obtained this report, so it was just another reason to sharpen our flying skills and be prepared for the worst.

One of the guys in my squadron was "Mouse" Albert. I guess the name originated because "Mouse" was so short. I often wondered how his feet ever reached the rudder pedals of his Hellcat. I asked Albert how he ever got through the initial flight physical because they specified a minimum height. Mouse replied, "I was just over the minimum by about a quarter of an inch. I had to stretch out my neck and cheat a little by standing on my toes just enough to pass the test. The pharmacist mate who measured me just rolled his eyes and said, 'You're borderline, kid, but you look like you could be a tough son of a bitch. Good luck.' "

I liked Mouse. He was the kind of guy who always built your morale, always had a smile, and always was willing to hear your troubles. Mouse was a funny guy. When he would prepare for a combat flight, he would wear two straps across his chest with two 45s mounted in a holster with the rest of the belt just loaded with cartridges. You would swear he intended to take on the whole Japanese Army single-handed. That wasn't all. Besides the arsenal of guns, Mouse carried four 10-inch knives, two sewn in his pant legs and two sewn in sleeves. We used to tell him, "Mouse, if you ever have to bail out, you'll sink like a rock." And, "if that don't kill you, if you land in the water, you'll drown first." Often I would fly off the wing of Mouse's plane.

There was no doubt that this little guy was ready to tangle with any enemy who got in his way. Mouse, besides being short, sported a goatee. If anybody ever looked like a renegade, Mouse was it. It was guys like Mouse who just seemed to help lessen the tension of daily events.

Each day it seemed that overall activity was beginning to step up. There were fewer bull sessions. Everyone down to the lowest rank seaman seemed to take on a more serious attitude. We all knew the big event was about to begin.

It was around 11 o'clock on this particular morning when, over the loudspeaker, the ship's captain shouted, "Now hear this! Now hear this! Communications from headquarters; United States Pacific Fleet has just announced that Japan has agreed to an unconditional surrender. Two major industrial cities (Hiroshima and

Lieutenant (j.g.) Walter H. Albert.

Discussing combat fighter tactics aboard the USS Saratoga.
Fletcher second from right.

Air Group Eight aboard the USS Bennington, South Pacific.

Nagasaki) along the main coast of Japan have been devastated by the use of a highly secret weapon called the Atom Bomb."

Not having heard of the Atom Bomb, we wondered just what it was. All we were told was that the force of the Atom Bomb was so great that one bomb literally destroyed an entire city. While at Saipan we never realized that less than seven miles away on the island of Tinian, the B-29s would soon change warfare forever.

Following this announcement, there was a sigh of relief that affected everyone there. Except for the splashing waves against the side of the ship's hull, there seemed to be an eerie shroud of silence after the two cities were leveled by the two bombs. No one expected the war to end so abruptly.

For the next ten days or so, we slowly cruised into the waters of Japan. After receiving orders from the Pacific Fleet Commander, the USS Bennington slipped quietly into Tokyo Bay where we anchored. With us was the now famous USS Missouri, where the final surrender documents were signed.

After a few days, the ship pulled anchor and launched several of our fighters. During this brief period, I was one of the fortunate few who was catapulted off the Bennington to carry out air patrol flights over the Japanese mainland. During these flights we would swoop down just above the rooftops to get a good look at the villages. As soon as we started down, the Japanese, not fully knowing the status of the war, would scramble for cover like a bunch of field mice.

As we reanchored in Tokyo Bay, the skipper announced that we would be able to go ashore in small groups. My turn came, and after exchanging United States currency for Japanese yen (the exchange value of which I really did not understand), we boarded the shuttle boat for the trip to shore.

Reaching shore, anxiety began to build within me. What were the Japanese like? Would I be able to communicate with them? Is it possible that they would try to lead us astray in an effort to kill us?

Joining a few of my squadron buddies, Mouse Albert, Screech Letts, Papa Stokes and a few others, we disembarked on the docks of Tokyo Bay. I'll never forget that chilled look in the Japanese people's eyes as we walked by them. The smaller children would swing way around us. I guess they thought we were foreign warriors just waiting for a chance to kill them.

Armed with our usual body weapons, we headed up the road in Tokyo just as though we were walking through central Manhattan. Typical skyscrapers of sorts loomed above us. Luckily, Tokyo was one of the major cities spared by the bomb. With little visible devastation because of the sudden surrender, our first excursion went reasonably smoothly. Having an abundance of cigarettes, candy, and other goodies, it was soon easy to barter for small gifts made from pure silk and teakwood boxes and other quality homeland gifts.

I believe it was the third day when we returned to Tokyo Bay. I can remember a young Japanese child walking towards me with this oversized basket that I at first thought was full of clothes. Soon, it became apparent that this child was trying to trade a basket full of low value currency in exchange for a cigarette, which I presumed was for his elderly grandpa sitting on a wooden bench just across the street. It was apparent to me that this old man was using the child for some devious errand.

A basket of money for a pack of cigarettes seemed to me like a good deal. So after the trade, I took my basket of currency back to the Bennington and dumped its contents on the wardroom dining table.

After sorting the bills, I proceeded down to the Foreign Exchange Officer, thinking all the time that I had just pulled off the biggest financial deal west of San Francisco. Soon I saw this wide grin come across the Exchange Officer's face. Laughing like a hyena, he said, "Son, you just got screwed, blued and tattooed. This currency exchanges at the rate of one hundred bills for a half cent each. It's less work for me if you just march your ass on deck and throw this junk to the wind."

Well, this knocked the huge financial coup about to be made right out to sea. When I finally overcame this royal screwing, I vowed that if I got ashore again, I was going to make an effort to look up this kid so I could kick him squarely right in the ass. But we didn't get ashore again, and even if we had, the odds of finding the young entrepreneur were remote.

By the end of that week, the skipper told us that Fighting Squadron Eight had received new orders to steam back to San Francisco via Pearl Harbor. This was welcome news. Our grinding vigilance of day-to-day Air Group Eight patrols over the past several months left a few of us visibly strained from the war and just waiting for a signal to return to the States.

Often I have been asked, "Just what goes on in your mind during a dogfight?" Let me say that all through our combat training we became constantly mindful of the many dangers that lay ahead. It was during that period that each of us developed the self-control so necessary to handle almost any life-threatening situation. While at sea aboard ship, our idle hours were occupied to keep our minds free from the events of war around us. Our daily briefing in the ready room kept us abreast of the nearest conflict by letting us in on anticipated enemy activities that could threaten the task force's operational position.

Task forces armed with several carrier air groups provided the aerial support for the Marines throughout their invasion. Pilots were often called on to take out enemy installations that threatened the progress of advancing marines. These beachhead invasions attracted enemy aircraft from other nearby enemy controlled islands and, in many instances, enemy carriers located several miles from our fleet would spring into action and launch Japanese aircraft to counter the Marine island offensives. Long before they reached their target, the United States Task Force carrier pilots would have to intercept the enemy and engage in an air battle to destroy as many enemy aircraft as possible before they reached the marine assault beachhead. The greatest tension built just hours before a confrontation was about to happen. The ready room became active with defensive strategies for protecting the fleet. The first shock to the pilot came when the General Alarm sounded throughout the ship, a shrieking series of clangs that sent our blood pressure off the charts. Adrenaline surges throughout the body, generating an exhilaration of muscle twitching with stepped-up activity while climbing into your Hellcat for that catapult blastoff should your plane be forward of the bridge. Once you're airborne circling your ship, tension subsided as you waited for your respective group leaders and wingmen to take up their protective positions. Within minutes the squadron began to achieve altitude advantage and to fly outward toward the anticipated zone of potential incoming enemy aircraft. The plan was to meet enemy aircraft outside the ship's range of antiaircraft fire and to engage the enemy on a one-on-one basis to prevent his entering this critical antiaircraft zone. Should enemy planes succeed in breaking through this outer combat defense, which often occurred, the ship's antiaircraft guns took over to destroy the enemy aircraft before reaching our invading forces.

Just before combat, flight formations close ranks for coordinated protection. At the moment an enemy sighting is reported, voice chatter among flight leaders establishes what potential targets to pursue. When the air battle begins, your eyes scan the skies in every possible direction. It's like a boxer sitting on his stool just waiting for that bell to ring, a signal sending him into the combat arena. When a target is spotted, a thumbs-up is given to your respective wingman, who drops slightly back to protect your rear while you engage your enemy. Combat can last thirty to fifty minutes. Almost every violent climbing and diving maneuver is enacted to gain an altitude advantage. There's more exhilaration when you can roll over into a dive and find the enemy moving into your sight and into position to depress your trigger finger, hoping for that instant kill. Once any of the enemy broke through our fighter defenses, we could no longer enter the antiaircraft controlled airspace. While engaged in dogfights, other Grumman Hellcats and the Marine Corsair gull-wing fighters were making low-level strafing attacks over enemy-bunkered installations that were raising havoc with our invading troops. Finally, when the skies cleared, the air group would rendezvous and wait to be cleared through the ships' central zone. Landing on

Fighting Squadron Eight on patrol, South Pacific.

a carrier following such an encounter took every bit of concentration to achieve a controlled carrier landing. More often than not Hellcats would return with slight control damage from taking a hit, making it still more difficult to execute a precision landing when nerves and tensions were at a feverish pitch. A double shot of whiskey often followed a safe return. Then again, I can tell you there were others who would take that double shot at the sound of a general alarm. It seems strange but I can honestly say that those who took a shot of whiskey before climbing into their fighters were guys whom I could close up on within five feet and feel safer than those without the alcohol. Human life is precious. Knowing many who did not return still is emotional for me and to most veterans.

Departing Tokyo Bay for our return to the United States, the carrier had no more than just passed out of the entrance when Commander Duke, the skipper of Fighting Eight, passed the word over the speaker to launch the fighters again. Over the next two hours, I circled south of Tokyo to get one last look at the atomic bomb devastation. The sight was enough to turn your stomach. You just knew thousands of small defenseless children were killed or maimed for life. Turning back to the carrier, I said one last prayer and counted my blessings that this violent act was not the result of my doing.

After several days at sea, the Hawaiian Islands once again came into view. Word spread that we were going to Pearl Harbor for some fresh supplies before departing for San Francisco. We had little to do other than to relax on the carrier deck bathing in the sun and trying to recollect the accomplishments of our Fighting Squadron.

Shortly after arriving back at Pearl Harbor on Hawaii, I learned one of my female classmates worked at the hospital. Robena Hyde was one of the popular girls in my class and a good friend who often helped me with my homework the year before graduation in 1940. Robena was then a nurse, and I was lucky to catch up with her over the phone. The next two evenings we spent in the Officer Club lounge just talking about our good old school days and the dances we often attended.

Before I could really start to unwind, we were directed to return to the USS Bennington to make preparations for our final leg home to San Francisco. After departing, we all got one last glimpse of the famous Diamond Head.

After several days at sea, we were all summoned up on the flight deck to receive our grand welcome at the Golden Gate Bridge, the same bridge we flew under and then were fined 800 bucks!

People along the banks were waving flags, blowing horns, and shooting off firecrackers. Alongside our carrier were several tugboats escorting us into the Alameda Naval docks, shooting streams of water high into the air to add to the celebration of our arrival.

America, my homeland, never looked better.

9

Returning Home

My experience in the Pacific War was surely reflected in my attitude. I came home hardened and took my day-to-day life much more seriously.

Of course, Dad and Mom were elated to see me home safe again. In the front yard sat Dad's old Chevy, "Blue Beetle," repaired after my crackup following graduation as a naval aviator. Without a doubt, Dad was reluctant to give me the car keys again. Sure, I made a mistake and fell asleep at the wheel with a girl friend from high school. But I was Dad's first-born son, the one who went to war. I came home, alive! — and in one piece. For the first time, I felt like a man, a real man. I was much more responsible. Dad must have sensed that when he welcomed me home. I suppose he figured that anyone who had been able to live through the Pacific War shouldn't be denied the car (especially since I was now his pride and joy). With a hint of a smile, he handed over the keys. His last words to me before leaving the house were, "Please don't crack up the car again. I won't be able to buy a new one for at least six months."

After about three weeks into my leave, I found myself missing the excitement of flying the Hellcats. But it was back to work. Bidding farewell to Mom and Dad again, I was off to San Diego. There, I joined our group of pilots who were waiting for permanent orders. Since several of my "Fighting Eight" friends were in the same group, we continued our daily flights to keep from becoming bored. To make it interesting, we often climbed over the mountain range just east of San Diego, then dove to the desert floor and proceeded to hedgehop over this sparse vegetation, burning up fuel at the rate of a gallon a minute.

It was in San Diego where we got our first look at a jet. It was called the Ryan "Fireball," a slick looking fighter that had a small jet engine in the tail and a conventional prop and engine in the nose. Being curious, we got permission to check out this experimental bird. After reading the checkout manual for a few days, we finally got a chance to fly our first jet, even though it was half jet and half prop.

After about a week's experience in the Fireball, a friend, Floyd Miles, decided that we should take off and see if we could find a commercial prop airline plane flying up the coast of California. During one of our aerial excursions, we found a commercial airlines plane at 12,000 feet. Dead set on having a little fun with the airline pilot, Floyd and I decided to pull up alongside of the airline plane in a safe formation. Waving at each other, Floyd and I agreed over the intercom that we would shut down our prop engine and fly only on the jet. While this was a relatively small, underpowered jet engine, we were sure we could keep up with the airliner. So we shut down the prop and feathered the blade at the same time kicking in the jet. It was obvious the airline pilots didn't know we had the jet, since it was hidden well within the tail of the fuselage. Well, if you could only see the faces of those airline pilots! It was as if they were saying, "What the hell is that! And how do they keep flying at our speed with the prop shut down?" Most of the guys on airliners had never heard of a jet, let alone seen one. After getting our kicks, we waved off and headed back to the base.

As I recall, the Thanksgiving holiday was already upon us. Late one evening, when sitting around the B.O.Q. bar bullshitting, my good friend, Vince, said to me, "Tomorrow is Thanksgiving Day. Let's grab a couple of Hellcats and fly up to my mom's house near San Francisco for Thanksgiving dinner. "Sounds good to me," I said to Vince. It was much better than hanging around the base over the holiday and being bored. With that, Vince contacted his mom, who was delighted to have her famous son home for Thanksgiving.

At seven o'clock sharp on Thanksgiving morning in November of 1945, Floyd, Vince, and I fired up our Hellcat engines and flew north, up the California mountain ranges to Moffit Naval Air Station just outside the Frisco area. Swooping down over Moffit Field (a relatively inactive airfield), we flew low over the end of the runway and peeled off one by one in a colorful wingover to impress Vince's old man. After landing and taxiing up to the Operations Office, we spotted Vince's dad frantically waving at his hotshot son. After securing the planes and completing the introductions, Vince's dad drove us in his beat-up old Chevy (much like my dad's "Blue Beetle") back to his house.

Vince's mom knew how to cook a Thanksgiving dinner second only to my mom's. What a terrific meal it was. After about an hour of family chatting, it was getting close to 2:30 in the afternoon. Bidding the family farewell, Vince's dad drove us back to Moffit Field for the return trip to San Diego. Just after getting airborne, Floyd called on the intercom. "Let's push these Cats a little so we can be on time for a Thanksgiving dinner back in San Diego. If we get back before 6 p.m., we can celebrate again at the Officers Club." Raising our thumbs in agreement, we bent the throttle on the way back and coasted into the San Diego Naval Air Station at 5:35 p.m., took a quick shower, and started the festivities all over again for the second time that day.

A few weeks later, we received our new orders. This time, Vince, Miles, and I were breaking up. My orders called for me to report to the Grosse Isle Naval Air Station in Michigan after a few weeks leave, which took me through Christmas of 1945. During this leave, a few of my hometown friends got together over the weekend and canvassed most of the bars in the rural New Jersey County of Sussex. It was in one bar, then out the door to the next, looking for action as most servicemen back from the war were then doing.

First evening ashore after arriving home at San Francisco on USS Bennington. Cousin Robert Salvas, Lieutenant, U.S. Army (left); Charles J. Fletcher, Ensign, U.S. Navy (right).

We were in a bar in Newton, the seat of Sussex County, when one of the guys said, "Hey, I think there's a square dance at the Hamburg High School. Let's shoot over there." As I remember, this fourteen-mile trip was made in record time, and I wonder how we ever got there alive and in one piece. Being on leave, I was all dressed up in my snappy navy blue officer's full-dress outfit.

Arriving at the school, the auditorium was alive with square dance music. I stuck my head in the door and before I knew it, this cute little Slovak gal grabbed me by the arm. Next thing I knew I was in the middle of the dancing. Well, as it happened, I got a crush on this gal and asked if I could stop by her house in Franklin on Christmas Eve, if she had no objections. I truly believe she doubted I was serious.

It was snowing lightly on Christmas Eve. It was a classic Curier and Ives Christmas setting of snowflakes and a soft white blanket topping the rooftops and treetops. Once more I had to ask Dad for the old "Blue Beetle." Around 7:30 on Christmas Eve I drove to her house in Franklin, a distance of about two miles. I felt like the luckiest guy in the world. Dad always came through.

After driving slowly by her house three times, I finally mustered enough courage to park and knock on her door. With the snow fluttering down and joyous Christmas carols in the background, I sheepishly walked up the front steps, all decked out in my Navy blues, gold braid and all.

After knocking lightly a few times, I saw the door crack open, only to find this giant of a woman with her arms crossed looking at me as if to say, "What the hell do you want?" This six-foot, two-inch woman looked like she could pick me up by the collar. I told her I had promised her daughter, Helen, that I would stop by on Christmas Eve. She then became quite pleasant and finally let me in the house. Helen and I began dating during this leave, and I later corresponded with her frequently during my brief stay at the Grosse Isle Naval Air Station in Michigan.

I departed for Detroit, the first leg to Grosse Isle, then to the air base about two hours north of Detroit by car and bus. Around the Great Lakes, temperatures were well below zero, and I was less than happy about flying the Hellcat in subzero weather. As I look back, Grosse Isle seemed like the icebox of the world. Coming out of the warm Pacific and San Diego climates, this was a drastic change for me. This assignment, however, was nothing more than a holdover before the Navy decided what to do with me after the war. This was a time when thousands of servicemen were being discharged back to civilian status daily.

While at Grosse Isle, I was given the task of Base Flight Test Pilot, checking our planes coming out of annual maintenance. Most of these planes were Hellcats, but a few were Curtis dive-bombers. This assignment was never boring. You never knew exactly just how a plane would fly after a major overhaul. I had to put the planes through a series of routine checks to be certain maintenance was properly done before reassigning these aircraft back to the fighter squadrons.

The worst part was walking out to the planes at 6:30 in the morning and attempting to start the Pratt & Whitney R-2800 engines, capable of generating the same amount of horsepower. Most of the time it was ten to fifteen degrees below zero, cold enough to freeze the balls off a brass monkey. After using an auxiliary heater and making several attempts, the engines would usually fire up smoothly.

Once airborne, we would perform a dozen or more routine tests and cross-checks and then proceed to put these Hellcats through a series of aerobatic maneuvers second only to the Blue Angels, the crack Navy goodwill aerobatic team. Satisfied things were normal, we would generally fly up over the Canadian border about seventy-five to one hundred miles, seeking out and buzzing herds of deer before returning to the base. As I recall, there was little or no value to these flights, except as a mandatory maintenance test flight and, of course, maintaining our combat proficiency.

During this period, Helen and I wrote many letters. It was becoming obvious there was a mutual chemistry between us.

Several months later, sometime in late May of 1946, I received new orders to report to Fighting Squadron 20 stationed

Helen S. Fletcher, co-founder of Aerosystems Technology
and Secretary/Treasurer.

at Charleston, Rhode Island. This was welcomed since it was only
a stone's throw from northern New Jersey where I lived and
where I had more opportunities to see Helen.

Arriving at "Charlietown," as we called it, I was introduced
to all the other guys in the squadron, including their stodgy, smok-
ing skipper, Commander Anderson, who turned out to be a real
great guy. We got along just fine. The guys showed me real
respect because they knew I was just out of the Pacific. And, since
most of them were junior to me in rank, I'm sure they also realized that I had a lot of flying skills to teach them in our day-to-
day flight maneuvers.

While in Rhode Island, if I couldn't get down to see Helen
in Franklin, I would travel to Boston to see a gal I had met at the
Officer's Club, who was going to college at Wesley. However,
none of these Boston gals really interested me. Besides, this was
a busy and exciting time in my life, testing rehabilitated planes
and never knowing what to expect. It kept me sharp and on the
edge.

Some Saturday nights the guys in our squadron just stayed
on base and set up a couple of desk drawers at one end of the pool
table and shot craps all night until the wee hours of the morning.
Not versed in the art of gambling, I watched one of my close
friends for about a month while he made several thousand dollars.
Finally, I decided to play. Whatever he would bet, I would bet. I
ran up $2,300 before dropping out.

One day word came that the new Grumman Bearcats, the
next generation of fighters to replace the Hellcats, would arrive
soon. When they did, we were hot to get our hands on these
machines that were said to exceed Hellcat speed by some seventy-
five knots and could maneuver on a dime, making it, we then
thought, the world-class fighter of all time. These fighters were
flying engines that were slick, fast, and able to turn on a dime, a
major feature necessary to survive a good dogfight.

After about a month of comprehensive aerial training in the
Bearcat, we knew this was the Navy's ultimate weapon in the sky.
They were so easy to maneuver. There wasn't a fighter in the

world that could stand a chance in a real dogfight. This was the only plane I ever flew that I could take straight up and hang it on its prop like a helicopter. I would take it vertical into a climb until it could no longer climb, and then it would hang there at literally zero airspeed.

During the summer months when Helen played softball in the Franklin Girls Baseball League, I would get a small group of guys together, take the Bearcats off in formation, and head for Franklin. Within ten miles of Franklin, we were ready to push over in a shallow dive right over the mountain in North Jersey and head straight for Helen's ballpark. One mile out, the six of us would roll upside down and make a pass over her ball game about 300 feet or so above the ground. Looking back now, I know it was stupid. However, that's the way we lived all through the war years. Yes, we were young and foolish, but that's when you do such things.

Fear? Forget about it. Sometimes on the way down, our ground speed approached 500 miles per hour, the limit the aircraft manual said to stay below. To be sure, we avoided trouble at those excessive speeds since the new F8F Bearcats had an emergency flap that protruded out of their short wings. Its purpose was nothing more than an air brake, which provided precisely the right amount of drag to keep the plane below this critical high-speed range.

Despite all the fun and games, the days at Charlietown were primarily routine. The war was over, and most squadrons were put together to maintain our flying skills until the Navy decided when to retire us.

My most exciting experience at Rhode Island came one day when the entire Air Group 20 flew out to sea about 150 miles to wage simulated warfare on a fleet of U.S. destroyers. This group exercise involved about 125 planes made up of Curtis dive-bombers, torpedo bombers, and our fighters. This exercise went smoothly. However, on the way back to Charlietown Air Station, our Air Group noticed a huge column of smoke that appeared to come from the Air Station. As our Air Group approached the field, we soon learned that our B.O.Q. was on fire. More importantly, of the two units built like an extended condo, the one burning was where my room was.

By the time we landed and rushed to our quarters, the fire had raged through the building from one end to the other, consuming the rooms and all of its contents. My room near the end of the building was completely gutted. Four hours after the fire, each of us who had lived there went rummaging through the ashes hoping to find something left of our prize possessions. About all I was able to salvage were a few photos of my wartime experiences. Beyond that, I had lost everything I owned, right down to my underwear.

Because better than 60 percent of the Air Group had been located in this now fire-ravaged B.O.Q., the Secretary of the Navy flew the entire group down to Floyd Bennett Air Station in New York in a Navy transport. There, a Navy bus drove us into the city to be fitted with $2,000 worth of replacement clothing. Except for two days when we had nothing left but our flight suits, this turned out to be a pretty good deal. Two thousand dollars in 1945 went a long, long way. I got everything from slick dress blues to four additional full-dress uniforms with all necessary undergarments. After two days of this exclusive shopping, we returned with our new custom-fit uniforms looking better that ever. As many of us realized days later, however, one or two special things would come to mind that had been lost in the fire that could never be replaced at any price. For me, it was mostly a dozen objects or so acquired in Guam, Saipan, and Tokyo, including my photos that were my biggest irreplaceable loss.

It was about five months after joining the Fighting 20 at Charlietown Air Station that I received my third set of new orders, directing me to report to the Brunswick Naval Air Station in Maine. This was a transit base for the naval transports flying between the U.S. and England. The base also had two marine fighter squadrons stationed there, just hanging around much as I did at Charlietown.

Because of my expressed desire to someday become an aeronautical engineer, I was assigned duty as Commanding Officer in charge of Flight Test Engineering. Having had some experience at Grosse Isle, Michigan, this duty was natural and exciting for me because I would do the bulk of the test flying. Having two squadrons of Marine pilots stationed there gave me an opportunity to fly the Chance Vought Corsair, the famous gull wing fighter the Marines used for ground support strikes in the Pacific from our carriers.

After becoming familiar with the Corsair flying manual, I climbed in and attempted to fly one for the first time. Since the Corsair was a single seat fighter, the decision to part with the earth was mine alone. After starting up this tremendous engine and studying the array of flight instruments for better than five minutes, I finally found the courage to taxi this strange gull wing bird into position for takeoff. After getting my clearance from the Brunswick Tower, I slowly opened the throttle and began roaring down the runway.

The Corsair had such a long extended nose that it was difficult to see exactly where I was going. As soon as I could get enough airspeed, I lifted the tail off the ground and, upon reaching the speed of about 80 knots or 92 miles per hour, this beautiful machine leaped into the air like a jackrabbit. I was so impressed that for a moment I forgot to retract the landing gear. As soon as the gear was retracted into the wings, this bird picked up speed like a runaway train. Not having any special flight plan, I decided I would climb up to 10,000 feet and circle the Brunswick Air Base until I felt comfortable with this fascinating aircraft.

After two days of flying the Corsair, I felt confident enough to try some aerobatics. Much to my surprise, although the Corsair could go like a bat out of hell, it could not outmaneuver the Hellcat or the F8F Bearcat.

I recall making my first loop in the Corsair. As the nose came up over the horizon, it seemed as if it took forever to pull its long nose up and over the top of the loop. The Hellcats and Bearcats went up and over like a Ferris wheel. Although the Corsair was designated a fighter, it soon became apparent that its primary missions were to support ground troops during their assault and make high-speed strafing runs to eliminate tanks and ammo depots. These maneuvers never required making the high speed "G-loading" turns the Hellcats made in a serious dogfight. Our Hellcats were quick to respond to any Japanese aircraft fighter opposition against our Corsairs, assuring them of full air cover protection. Nevertheless, while I appreciated an opportunity to fly the famous Corsair, I still would rather fly the Grumman Hellcats because of their exceptional ability to outmaneuver the best the Japanese had to offer.

After several months at Brunswick Naval Air Station, I felt the urge to return to civilian life. I wanted to return to college in order to acquire a degree in aeronautical engineering, my lifelong ambition.

10

Return to
Civilian Life

$\mathcal{I}$ knew eventually it had to come, and it did – the day when I decided to end my active duty. It was a hard decision to make since I had learned to live with the daily dangers coupled with the glamour of being one of a chosen few who were considered to be the Navy's "cream of the crop." It had been the greatest learning experience of my life, one that prepared me to work as an inventor and entrepreneur in a ruthlessly competitive business environment.

I obtained a release from the Brunswick Commanding Officer and left for New York City where, along with many others, I was given a "job well done" letter from the Secretary of the Navy and an honorable discharge.

Boarding a bus out of New York City, I was still on terminal leave with pay for the next forty-five days to become acclimated to the civilian way of life. Of course, no one was happier about my return than Mom and Dad. After about two months of leave in which I roamed the local bars, got reacquainted with a few old girlfriends, and exchanged a few war stories with my buddies, I began to feel this lifestyle was a serious letdown after experiencing daily flights in the hottest aircraft the Navy ever produced. It's hard to explain what a depressing change it was, but I knew I had to accept the transition to civilian life if I wanted to pursue my dreams as an aeronautical engineer and designer.

Deciding to return to college, I discovered that during my delayed discharge, most of the colleges and universities had quickly filled up with other veterans using the GI Bill to finance their advanced education. It seemed as if everyone who had been discharged had decided to return to college.

Fortunately, I received word that I could enter the Academy of Aeronautics, which is now the Aeronautical Engineering Affiliate of New York University. The only trouble was I had already missed the September registration and could not start until the following year.

I decided to make a visit back to Franklin High School to see some of my old teachers. While there, my former principal asked me if I would be interested in a part-time teaching job. Not having anything more constructive to do, I was glad to accept this temporary job and felt it would put me back in the mood to condition myself to the college discipline I was about to face for the next three years.

I was assigned to teach Physics with Josephine McKeeby, a longtime friend. After several weeks, she allowed me to take over half of her class sessions. During the next several months, the students, who respected me as a seasoned Naval aviator, enlisted me to conduct classes in the theory of flight. This was a great uplift since I was no longer flying. And as part of this program, several students combined the classes with Advanced Model Airplane Building, for which I had considerable experience from my high school days.

About halfway through the school year, I was invited to remain active with the Navy as a "weekend warrior" in a Naval Reserve Program at Floyd Bennett Field in Jamaica, New York, a program that gave me a renewed opportunity to continue flying those terrific Hellcats. This program called for spending one full weekend a month flying with a reserve fighter squadron to maintain flying proficiency skills. This activity gave me a whole new upbeat outlook on life while, at the same time, I was enjoying a brief return to formal education as a part-time teacher.

Having access again to Naval aircraft, I often found one of my local buddies who drove down to Floyd Bennett with me where I was able to reserve a SNJ, better known as a two-seated Navy fighter trainer. The North American SNJ was a great airplane to practice aerobatics. With a local friend in the passenger seat, I flew back into North Jersey where Franklin was located and then proceeded to ring the hell out of the SNJ with every known aerobatic maneuver. After a couple of months, just about every friend I knew as a war veteran got wind of my escapades and wanted me to take them for a ride. There were a few times when I took it upon myself to swoop down over the town and then circle up over Mom and Dad's house before climbing out for a return trip to Floyd Bennett Field in New York.

By late August of 1947, I knew it was time to experience college life at the Academy of Aeronautics at LaGuardia Field in New York. Over the next couple of weeks, I found an apartment about a mile from the Academy and settled down to a comprehensive academic program of aeronautical engineering.

Over the next three years, I was determined to complete my education. These were tough years. I had very little money, only that provided by the GI Bill for education subsistence, which I recall was about $25 a month, hardly enough to live on much less live it up. Weekends I returned home to Franklin where for at least two days a week Dad would support me with free room and board.

During those three years at the Academy, my girlfriend, Helen Swetz, and I dated frequently. By the second year, we were dating steadily, and I realized this was getting to be serious. We decided to become engaged.

During my time at the Academy of Aeronautics, I became interested in the comprehensive aeronautical design project the school had developed. After the second year, as a test of our design capabilities, each of us was given the task of designing a complete airplane from start to finish. To achieve this, we would have to use our knowledge gained earlier in our classes to determine the structural strength of the aircraft, assuming it was being subjected to a variety of high-stress loads typical of what would be expected for the type of aircraft we selected to design. I elected to design a twin-engine executive aircraft capable of carrying two pilots and four passengers.

Although this was an extraordinary challenge, I was able to produce a beautiful aircraft that had all the features of corporate luxury. My instructor called me in one day and suggested that this was one of the finest executive aircraft ever designed at the school. I must confess that this project pumped my ego to where I began to get visions of someday becoming a major aircraft manufacturing entrepreneur.

It was at this time that flying saucer sightings were being reported all up and down the northeastern coast from Boston to Atlantic City. Our squadron was placed on alert to investigate these reports because of the numerous "sightings" in the Westchester area of New York.

I was just starting my class one Friday afternoon at the Academy when I was summoned to the Superintendent's office. School officials had received a call from Floyd Bennett Field ordering me to report immediately to my squadron commander.

I arrived at the field around 3:30 that Friday afternoon. As I walked into the Ready Room, a place where preflight briefings were made, our C.O. was at the podium explaining what our mission would be. Next to him was our Communications Officer who had received call after call from individuals around the metropolitan New York City area.

Things seemed crazy! People were seeing round objects just about everywhere. These bizarre "sightings" were all over the east coast by noon on Saturday. By 1:30 that Saturday afternoon, our fighter squadron was split into flight sections of two pilots; each was designated a quadrant of 10 degrees around the compass. This pattern of flight assured us of full regional coverage. My section was northwest between 300 and 310 degrees, which placed our patrol just north of my hometown of Franklin.

Because of the frantic number of calls coming into Floyd Bennett Field, we took these sightings seriously. From around

Floyd Bennett Naval Air Station, NY. Weekend Warrior, 1948.

1:45 p.m. that Saturday until well after midnight Sunday morning, my wing man, Bill Johnson, and I flew two-hour legs in our 300 to 310 degree segment with a 30-minute break every flight. By 2:45 Sunday morning, we were exhausted. But not a single pilot in our entire squadron in all that time of approximately fourteen hours reported what was believed to be a flying saucer! By 2:30 a.m. our skipper was so exhausted that he called off all further flights until 9 o'clock Sunday morning.

After a brief and uneasy sleep, we grabbed a hot cup of coffee and a Danish and returned to the Ready Room to hear our briefing for the day. By this time it was a joke among our pilots who had flown half the night before. While sitting in the Ready Room waiting for our skipper to arrive, each of us exchanged stories, but none of us had encountered a sighting.

At 8:45 Sunday morning, the skipper showed up with an armful of paper plates (probably 250 or more). Standing before the podium, the skipper said, "Gentlemen, let's give these New Yorkers something to talk about." With that, he began passing out twenty-five or thirty paper plates to each pilot. Immediately, everyone burst out laughing. Then the skipper said, "Each of your groups will retain your sectors. However, as we enter the New York City area from about five miles out at an altitude of seven thousand feet, I will give the signal to roll open your canopies. And, when I say go, throw the damn paper plates out into the air stream so they will drift over part of Long Island and the City of New York."

With that offbeat order, we fired up our Hellcat engines and, one group at a time, took off to our assigned quadrant. Again, after two hours of straining our eyes looking for those annoying "reported sightings," we finally rendezvoused just north of Westchester. Twenty planes in all formed a large circle formation.

The skipper ordered a reduction in speed to 110 knots with our wheels and flaps down to maintain that slow speed. Within minutes, the skipper broadcast over the intercom to our planes, "Get ready! Now! Throw the damn saucers out." As the white plates began their descent over the New York City area, all twenty

Hellcats scattered in every direction to mask the project from being identified as the source of the saucers. As we turned away from the paper plate drop area, looking back, we saw a wide field of glistening disks fluttering in the sun. What a spectacle to behold!

After we made the drop, I seriously wondered if we would get caught in this scheme. I had had my ass reamed once for flying under the Golden Gate. I wasn't really interested in having this happen again. However, before we had approached Floyd Bennett Field for our landing, I had convinced myself. What the hell! They couldn't discharge me. I was already a civilian only serving weekend reserve duty.

As we entered the Ready Room, the radios were crackling away with reports of numerous sightings over the New York area. None of us was able to keep a straight face as the area went wild with paper plate reports. I was just hoping the event would go away.

Since it was Sunday afternoon, each pilot checked out and headed for home. That evening, the New York papers carried the sightings over the eastern part of Long Island. The drop was timed in such a way as to be sure the plates drifted out to sea to destroy the evidence. To this day, I don't believe anybody except our pilots knew of our participation in that event.

Back at the Academy of Aeronautics, I continued being deeply engrossed in the design and development of my twin-engine executive six-passenger plane, which I took on as a final project a year before graduation. Always having a love and special talent for artistic design, this work truly offered me an opportunity to create an aircraft purely from my own imagination. I believe it was during this period of free engineering thinking that I cultivated a love for inventing things.

As I approached graduation, I decided to write a technical paper for presentation at graduation called the aerodynamics of the "Flying Saucer," a fitting subject.

While at the Academy, Helen and I got together almost every weekend. I couldn't wait to leave on Friday afternoon after classes for that hour-and-a-half trip back to Mom and Dad's house in Franklin. By then I had enough cash stashed away to make a down payment on one of the new Chevys that was coming on the market. Having a single girlfriend kept me well focused between enjoying weekends and the pressures of rigorous study at the Academy.

My final project was to provide a five-minute dissertation on my chosen subject – "The Aeronautical Feasibility of Flying Saucers" – to all of the visitors and students of the graduating class. Mom, Dad, and Helen were there. Graduation day finally became a reality. In the late spring of 1950, I had reached my goal of becoming an Aeronautical Engineer.

11

My First Job

Shortly after graduating from the Academy of Aeronautics, I
spent the next several weeks looking for my first job as an
aeronautical engineer. I lucked out when I was offered a job in a
small company in North Jersey, Marotta Engineering, which had
gotten in on the ground floor developing sophisticated control
valves for the Viking Rocket. Its rocket engine was being developed by Reaction Motors, the first rocket motor company
engaged in the new field of rocket engineering. I was given my
first job designing extremely complex control valves that were
under contract to the Navy. After about two months of this activity, I began submitting several new designs to my boss and soon
learned he wasn't happy about my effort to invent new concepts
that were in competition with his own ideas. I suspected he was
concerned about my ability to create valves that could make his
design concepts look obsolete. His animosity over my design ver-
sions that I believed were superior to his made working with him
more and more difficult.

One Monday morning, I was summoned into the office of
Patrick Marotta, the founder of the company and the Chief Executive Officer. As I entered, I could see by the frown on his face
that there was something wrong. Turning his embarrassed head
away, Pat said, "Sit down, my boy. I have to tell you something.
Your boss feels uncomfortable about your inventive talent and has

asked me to terminate you. I regret having to do this. However, my chief designer, Carl, has been with me a long time and, therefore, I have no other alternative but to let you go." Since this was my first professional engineering job, I was deeply hurt. There was not much I could do about it, so I packed my personal belongings in a little box and headed for home.

My first thought was wondering what my dad would say about my being canned after just three months on the job. However, after explaining the situation to him, I was surprised at his response: "If that was the way your ingenuity was being suppressed, you should have quit first." Thinking about it, I began believing it was in my best interest to be fired, although I must admit, it was extremely hard to accept.

After a couple of weeks, I began looking at employment ads in two leading aeronautical publications, *Aviation Week* and *Aero Digest*. I learned that a new company in Morton, Pennsylvania, called Piasecki Helicopter, was looking for a flight test engineer. This job excited me because if I were to get it, I would be back in the mainstream of general aviation.

I traveled to Morton where I checked in for employment. I filled out the typical employment application and waited for my interview. I quickly learned that my naval aviation pilot experience coupled with my aeronautical engineering education was just exactly what they were looking for. The most difficulty I had was explaining my departure from Marotta. With some apprehension I told the interviewer exactly what happened, and fortunately, they not only accepted my explanation, but I sensed they had a real interest in my ability to create new and interesting ways to make things better with innovative designs.

As it was, I left Marotta making $47 a week and was offered the job as flight test engineer at Piasecki earning $110 a week. I couldn't believe it! Being able to more than double my salary from Marotta Engineering really built my confidence over the disappointment of being fired at the outset of my career.

I settled down comfortably in my new job. Piasecki was then just beginning to flight-test what was known as ground resonance frequency phenomena on the Navy Model HUP, a tandem rotor helicopter designed for Naval carrier rescue. These tests were especially interesting because when you hover a helicopter close to the ground where the wheels just touch the ground lightly and sporadically, a vibration begins to develop in the fuselage that gets out of control. If you continue to induce this condition, the increased vibration amplitude can twist the helicopter fuselage in half. One of the test programs did create such a violent vibration buildup that it severely damaged the landing gear and mainframe, causing it to twist out of alignment.

This test program led to my most important contribution to the field of aeronautics and played a major role in my life a few years later. But that gets ahead of my story.

After about six months of working on the Piasecki helicopter development program and traveling from Morton, Pennsylvania, home to Franklin weekends to spend time with Helen, we both decided after some three and a half years of courtship that it was time to consider marriage. We announced our engagement and started to make plans for the big day. Right before this giant step into marriage, I caught the flu – at least the Philadelphia doctors thought it was the flu. For over three months, I traveled back and forth between Philadelphia and Franklin through Thanksgiving and Christmas fighting this physically debilitating condition. After the New Year in 1951, I became so weak that the doctors admitted me into a suburban Philadelphia hospital in the hope of finding a cause for my illness.

Besides suffering from severe overall weakness, I would periodically experience shooting chest pains that made me think I was having a mild heart attack.

Though the doctor prescribed several newly invented antibiotics, the condition seemed to worsen. After nineteen long days in the hospital and numerous tests, the doctors couldn't find any specific cause for my illness. They discharged me from the hospital and recommended treatments at home.

Helen and I decided we had better plan for the wedding for March 31, 1951. I was still very ill only two-and-a-half months from the scheduled wedding date, wondering each day if I would live long enough to meet the challenge. Over the two months prior to the wedding, I felt a wee bit better from time to time, but never confident enough to face the wedding day. For the final days before the wedding, I suffered each day just a little bit less, then a little bit more, until at last, March 31st — the big day had arrived.

Of course, all the while this was going on, Helen had completed the wedding plans. The reception was scheduled to take place in a small country hotel north of Franklin in the town of Sussex, ten miles from the Catholic Church where we were to be married. Several of my high school friends were still around, so we picked several to participate. Now when I look back, I truly believe that this illness was largely triggered by a daily anxiety attack that seemed to start minutes after awakening in the morning.

On the day of the wedding, I was having a hard time. The pains in my body were severe at times, but I tried to pass it off. As I started for the church, I prayed I would hold up and not show the physical discomfort I was experiencing. Finally, down the aisle I walked. I can recall my attempts to remain calm. Nevertheless, I felt a cold bead of sweat on my brow minutes before Father Steve, the local Catholic priest, completed the ceremony. Somehow as I walked back up the aisle, I felt a sigh of relief flow from my body and, with a fake smile on my face, I realized that I had survived this ordeal.

Within minutes, we were off to the reception at the Sussex Inn. Helen, being of Slavic descent, had many friends of the family in attendance. The band we selected was able to play a variety of polkas to liven things up.

For as long as I can remember, this was the first time my dad really let loose. Dad never drank. At least I never saw him inebriated. But this time, I believe he had had a bit too much. He had so much that my younger brother, Bobby, at about twelve years of age, was so embarrassed by Dad's condition that Ray, my oldest brother, had to take Bobby home.

After about six hours of the wildest party I had attended in years, Helen and I, remaining until the end, left for New York. We stayed there the first evening of our marriage before flying to Miami the following morning.

Arriving in Miami before noon, we rented a car and drove directly to our luxury hotel out on Miami Beach. There, things were going along just fine. I started to feel better than usual, basking in the beach sun over the next three days.

Then we decided to take a short walk down the beach to take in a few of the sights. We stopped at a food stand, which was selling hot dogs marinated in beer. At the time, it didn't sound so bad, so we both had a hot dog and walked back to the hotel. It was not more than fifteen minutes after arriving that my stomach started to turn upside down. I quickly broke out into a cold sweat, threw up several times, and became so weak that I was forced into bed.

Concerned, Helen immediately called for a house physician who diagnosed my condition as a severe case of ptomaine poisoning from the hot dog. After recommending complete bed rest and giving me a heavy dose of penicillin, he left me with the heaves and as weak as a kitten.

It seemed he wasn't gone thirty minutes when Helen started to develop the same symptoms. Soon she began to throw up the same way I had and within minutes was weak and totally miserable. Crawling over to the hotel phone, I called the house physician a second time, who immediately diagnosed Helen with the same ailment.

Here it was our honeymoon and we were both flat on our backs, so pathetically sick we couldn't even get out of bed for the next three days. There was a brief spell when I thought we were both going to die. Not being flush with cash, we had to pay the doctor $100 for each call and another $100 each for the shot of penicillin. So it cost us a whopping $400 just to recover.

As we slowly regained our composure from this dual physical illness, we finally spent the last six or seven days lying on the beach regaining our strength. I couldn't help recall those final words at the altar, "in sickness and in health." Those few days of incapacitation were our first trial of living up to those sacred words.

Winding up our stay at Miami Beach, we set out to board an Eastern Airlines plane for our flight back to New Jersey. Following a short visit with our parents, we headed off to Swarthmore, Pennsylvania, where we rented a room from the mother of one of my friends who also worked at Piasecki Helicopter. There, in our newly rented room in the small, wealthy town of Swarthmore, we began our new married life.

Helen, who had always worked for an insurance company or a bank, soon decided to see Piasecki Helicopter about a job. Fortunately, she was hired in their Accounting Section, which added to our income.

My illness continued well beyond seven months until one day I experienced pain so bad that my doctor put me back in the hospital. Again, after numerous tests, everything showed normal, but believe me I was deathly ill. I was released after two weeks and again told it was all they could do for me. With this condition continuing month after month, and newly wed, I felt it was in our best interests to return to Franklin and seek out a new job close to our parents.

About a month later, I learned that Reaction Motors was hiring engineers, the same company for which Marotta Engineering was designing rocket fuel valves. I took a brief vacation from Piasecki Helicopter and arranged an appointment with Reaction Motors, one of the most advanced rocket development companies in the United States back in the early 1940s and 1950s. During my interview I discovered that Reaction Motors was interested in hiring an engineer with an aeronautical engineering background to pursue development of a rotor blade tip rocket for the Sikorsky Helicopter boost power emergency rescue system. Because of my extensive background as a Navy pilot coupled with my recent Piasecki experience in aeronautical engineering, my interviewer told me that I was the perfect candidate for this development project. I was hired.

Before the week was over, I resigned from Piasecki Helicopter and transferred my naval reserve base from Willow Grove

Naval Air Station to Floyd Bennett Naval Air Station in New York, to join a fighter squadron there. I decided to continue in the Naval Reserve as a weekend warrior flying Hellcats. New York was a better choice for me because of its proximity to Franklin. As fate would have it, early in my new position at Reaction Motors, word began to leak out that the war in Korea was beginning to escalate, possibly requiring the weekend warriors to be reactivated for full-time duty.

While waiting for a decision to return to active duty as a member of a Naval Reserve fighter squadron, I made daily trips to Reaction Motors Engineering Department, which was perched up on a mountain just east of the Army's Picatinny Arsenal, where Reaction Motors leased a series of rocket engine test stands. At this site I ran static tests on a man-made rig with a two-bladed rotor on the top of the frame. The end of the rotor blades provided a place to mount these little rotor-blade rocket engines no larger than a pack of cigarettes. Each day I would mount two small engines on the helicopter rotor blades. Each engine had a shell that resembled that of a twenty-gauge shotgun. Except instead of gunpowder, we packed the shell with alternating wire mesh disks made of stainless steel and pure silver. Our research taught us that by using the small shell filled with stainless steel and silver disks, we could create a power source for this tiny engine. That power source was hydrogen peroxide (a liquid fuel). The hydrogen peroxide would decompose into a high velocity steam when forced through the rocket engine shell under high pressure.

By designing a rotor blade powered by this tiny engine, we would be able to generate a high-pressure hydrogen peroxide flow created from the centrifugal force of the rotating blades. This simple little process produced about 42 pounds of thrust per engine. When we measured the radius of the rotor and multiplied the 42 pounds of force, we ended up with the equivalent of about 140 extra horsepower for approximately four minutes using this powerful little engine at the tip of a three-bladed Sikorsky helicopter. This became the well-known and popular rescue vehicle used by the Marines during the Korean War.

As it was later proven, this little "rocket on a rotor" engine system rescued more that 103 military personnel from high in the Korean mountains at a height that would not allow a helicopter to hover and pick up a load for a lack of power from its own combustion engine. With this extra 140 horsepower added to the helicopter's engine, sufficient power was available just long enough to pick up a stranded soldier and fly away to safety.

I filed a U.S. patent with the help of the Office of Naval Research and was presented an award for this innovative aviation development. This patent became the property of the U.S. Navy.

12

Recalled Into Service

Shortly after Helen and I relocated back to the small community of Lake Mohawk, New Jersey (some five miles from Franklin), the Korean War was getting plenty of military attention. I was just getting up-to-speed in my new position at Reaction Motors, developing the new "rocket on rotor," when word came from the Naval Air Station in Atlanta, Georgia. With only seven days to settle my affairs, Helen and I had to drive down to Atlanta so I could report for full-time active duty.

Arriving in Atlanta, Helen went looking for an apartment on the outskirts of the Naval Air Station. I had to check into the dispensary for a flight physical. I had become quite concerned about my continuing illness over the previous year that at that time could not be cured. I thought that the doctors would find something wrong that would prevent me from continuing active duty. After a thorough physical, however, the doctor said everything checked out OK, except I seemed to have a lot of tension, which he attributed to my returning to an active flight status. His reassurance did boost my morale considerably, but I still experienced an unusual feeling of ill health from time to time.

I had no sooner arrived when I received word that I had been promoted to the rank of Lieutenant Commander and was assigned to a newly formed fighter squadron ready for advanced jet fighter training. I realized that once this initial jet training was completed, my next assignment would be aboard another aircraft carrier to join our fighter support over North Korea.

Knowing this would require a separation from Helen within two months, I decided to call a good friend, Admiral Fred C. Durrant, III, who was then commanding officer of the Naval Rocket Test Station in Lake Denmark, New Jersey. I told him I thought I could better serve the Navy in a position associated with the Bureau of Aeronautics in view of my aeronautical engineering credentials, as opposed to another tour as a fighter pilot in a hot jet for which I had relatively little training. Besides, I had already served well over nineteen months of flying off carriers in World War II. By 1951 I was no longer a kid looking for the thrills of combat, and having just been married a short time, I needed fighter squadron duty like I needed a bullet in the head.

Admiral Durrant agreed I would be wasting my engineering talent in a squadron, and he contacted the Pentagon to see if I could be reordered to a new position utilizing my engineering background. Two days later, Fred called me back in Atlanta and told me he was able to locate engineering assignments for three positions: Naval Representative at Cornell Aeronautical Research Laboratory in Buffalo, New York; Bureau of Aeronautics Eastern District Maintenance Representative (BAMR) with an office at the Naval Air Station in Norfolk, Virginia, as a liaison with the Bureau of Aeronautics in Washington, D.C.; and Bureau of Aeronautics representative for Grumman Aircraft Corporation, Bethpage, Long Island, New York. I told Fred I thought the BAMR position offered a real challenge because it was responsible for making sure the entire fleet of naval aircraft was properly maintained with the latest replacement components and updated technology.

In closing our conversation, Fred said, "You got it! Your new orders will be drafted within a few days." Still feeling some of the effects of my continuing illness, the news was great to hear for both of us. Before the month was over, Helen and I departed for the Norfolk Naval Air Station, and I was ready to take on my new assignment.

After a good night's rest at a hotel, I reported to the BAMR office located above the nearby naval aircraft overhaul and repair station. There I met my new commanding officer, Captain Henry Haselton, who briefly discussed with me just what my duties would entail. I was told I would be in charge of several civilian technical specialists who each had his own responsibility for some major function of all the aircraft in the fleet.

Captain Haselton assigned two airplanes to me. One was a Hellcat for short, fast trips and the second was a twin engine executive airplane for extended monthly trips to visit all the air stations on the eastern seaboard.

To welcome Helen and me aboard, Captain Haselton held a party in our honor that weekend to help us get acquainted with all BAMR personnel. What a party it was! There were several bowls of martinis, whisky sours, and manhattans with a spread of hors d'oeuvres. We both had one hell of a time. It was at this party that I had an opportunity to meet Chief Petty Officer Chuck Folles, who would be my pilot/copilot when we flew the twin engine Beechcraft. Chuck came up through the ranks and was one of the very few enlisted men who was given the privilege of upgrading to a full lieutenant during the Korean war. When the war was over, he reverted to chief petty officer but retained his flight status and his "Wings of Gold." Besides, Chuck was one of the best instrument-qualified pilots with whom I had ever had the privilege of flying.

For me, these monthly trips around the eastern seaboard presented some interesting weather problems, especially during the rough winter months. This gave me an opportunity for more "blind" instrument flying than I had ever experienced in the fighters.

Within a matter of months, we encountered an extremely severe snowstorm with icing conditions. While flying out of Niagara Falls, we ran into a severe icing condition that suddenly loaded up our wings and propellers with a dangerously heavy coat of ice. Over the next thirty minutes we exhausted all our deicing fluid, and flying became so critical that Chuck and I were forced to lower our altitude extremely close to the mountaintops in an effort to shake off the continuous buildup of ice. Speed began to reduce substantially to a point that unless the ice could be shaken off we would soon reach a slow flight stalling speed, leading to a spin and subsequent crash. Fortunately, as we approached our minimum safe altitude over the mountaintops, all hell broke loose as the ice melted from our props. It flung the ice against the fuselage with tremendous force as if we were being hit by a thousand bullets. Finally, we were able to regain our air speed and altitude as we ran into less severe weather. As things continued to improve on our way to Brunswick Naval Air Station, Chuck and I would alternate at pilot/copilot positions in order to help me gain the instrument experience I had lacked while flying fighters. This instrument flying was strictly by the book because our flights had to be coordinated with the commercial airlines.

After about three months flying at the BAMR office, I went to the dispensary once again. There, I talked over my continuing health problem with the chief surgeon who analyzed my condition. After reviewing my case, he said "You may be suffering from rapid adrenaline rush that is toxic to your blood and causing your pain." He noted most of my problem occurred within minutes after my morning alarm went off. Then the doctor said, "Try getting rid of the loud clock alarm and replace it with a radio with soft wake-up music."

What he thought was happening was that I would relate the clock alarm to the alarm I used to hear on the aircraft carriers when we were called to general quarters. This rush of adrenaline would poison my circulation system and cause the spells of pain. As a result of this clinical visit, a miracle was about to happen. After I replaced the alarm clock with a wake-up radio with soft music, my condition completely disappeared forever. What a relief this was! After more than fourteen months of this agonizing condition, it felt as if a heavy weight had been removed from my head.

The last week of each month called for Chuck and me, along with two or three of the civilian specialists, to fly down to Cherry

Point, North Carolina. One day while spending several hours there reviewing all the maintenance problems the marine fighter pilots were experiencing, I met Ted Williams, the famous Boston Red Sox player. Ted, a reserve fighter pilot when the Korean War broke out, had been called back about the same time I returned to active duty. Over the next three months, I saw Ted at the Officers Club in Cherry Point. Ted never acted as though he was above anyone else because of his Hall of Fame career as a ballplayer. As a Marine fighter pilot, he enjoyed being one of the boys. Several of his pilot associates often told me that Ted Williams was one of the most regular guys a squadron could ever have.

Our monthly trips up and down the eastern seaboard started from Norfolk, Virginia. Cherry Point, North Carolina, was our first stop. From there, we headed up to Akron, Ohio, then on to Columbus, Ohio, over to Niagara Falls Naval Air Station, on to Brunswick, Maine, then on to New York Floyd Bennett, next on to Lakehurst Naval Air Station in New Jersey, then back to Norfolk. The whole trip usually took about four days because sometimes we visited two stations the same day.

While at Brunswick, Maine, we borrowed a car from the navy base and drove out to a quaint seaport town about four miles from the air station. We would stop at this little fisherman's wharf and pick up two dozen lobsters. The owner wrapped each one in seaweed and placed them in a large plastic bag so we could carry them back to Norfolk in our twin-engine Beechcraft. Before we left our last station in North Carolina, we called ahead to the BAMR office. Arrangements were made with the Officers Club at Virginia Beach to be ready to cook the lobsters. Within an hour after arriving at the naval air station in Norfolk, the lobsters were driven to the Officers Club, where a seafood party had been prearranged. What a sumptuous feast we enjoyed. Every month we looked forward to this office party with the best fresh lobsters Maine could provide. I still think about it! These pound-and-a-half lobsters only cost us 50 cents each.

Except for this monthly jaunt, this job left me with considerable time back at Norfolk to sit around my office and pass my

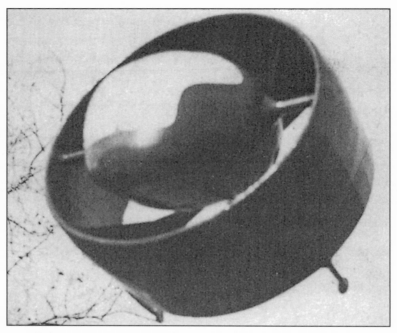

Fletcher Aerial Jeep, 1957, transitional flight, model view.

Fletchaire Aerial Jeep, model two.

time dreaming up new concepts for vertical lift aircraft. My employment at Piasecki Helicopter drove me to dream up wild concepts for developing a new breed of plane that would be able to take off vertically from a standstill, then quickly convert to high-speed level flight. Up until the time I left my employment at Piasecki, very little was done to attempt to create a new breed of hybrid aircraft that could achieve both vertical flight and horizontal flight, with the exception of the helicopter.

Helicopters were doing the job that airplanes could not. Unfortunately, they were not an easy machine to fly back in the early 1950s. After my brief employment as a Flight Test Engineer at Piasecki, I always referred to the helicopter as a vehicle with aerodynamic confusion. Helicopter blades beat the air with every rotation. At that time, they were noisy, relatively unstable, and the vibration was so severe that prolonged flying would wear out the seat of your pants.

Having this extra time available at BAMR in Norfolk, I thought there must be a better way to develop a hybrid vehicle that could fly both vertically and horizontally. After considerable daydreaming about this confounding hybrid vehicle, I created five distinct aircraft called "convertaplane" for their ability to fly both vertically at takeoff and then transpose into horizontal flight to achieve higher speeds. At this time (1951-52), the Army began to look for a vehicle to do just that, yet small enough that individual soldiers could possibly fly one. This led to my creation of the "Aerial Jeep" and a second vehicle which I dubbed the "Glide-mobile" — a waterborne vehicle that would fly just off the water yet fly at extremely high speeds, as opposed to the dangerously slow assault boats used to transport troops and weapons ashore during combat beachhead landings. Both of these aircraft appeared to offer real potential. To protect those original designs, I prepared U.S. patent applications for them.

While in Norfolk, Helen and I lived in a small apartment where I found room to do aircraft design. To find an adequate drafting board, I purchased a smooth plywood door and mounted it on the wall next to our bed, so whenever I got a good idea, all

I had to do was to hinge the door up level and drop a handmade leg to support the door. This made for a good-sized drafting board.

Ultimately, I became obsessed with trying to invent a new breed of aircraft that had the ability to fly both off the ground like a helicopter and to convert into a relatively high-speed airplane. I would often dream of these new vehicles that I couldn't get out of my mind while sleeping, so I awoke in the early hours of the morning and turned on a dim light to allow me to sketch these unconventional aircraft that were still fresh in my mind. After catching a few winks of sleep following these drafting episodes, I would evaluate the technical merits of these machines the next day, and if I found them practical enough to achieve my convertaplane goal, I resketched these aircraft concepts onto patent drawing bristol board paper to prepare for filing the patent.

Because patents were so expensive, I purchased a few books that described how to file patents without a lawyer. To assist me, Helen bought an inexpensive typewriter and, in the evenings would type the patent specifications in the form of a rough draft patent. Over the next four years, seven of these designs were approved for patents — all without ever using an attorney. Two patent applications became historical documents. One was the "Aerial Jeep" and the other was the "Glidemobile."

As my BAMR assignment wound down in late 1953, I had acquired sufficient patent filings and had developed a number of friends at Piasecki, as well as admirals and captains at the Office of Naval Research who strongly believed the vertical lift convertaplane concepts had real merit. So I decided that as soon as my tour of duty was over, I would seek out venture capital to start a new aircraft company. I would name it Fletch-Aire, Inc.

When it came time to leave my BAMR duty in Norfolk, I requested permission to go to helicopter school in Pensacola, Florida. My fanatical interest in vertical flight was stronger than ever. I believed that learning to fly a variety of naval helicopters would condition me to better understand the theory of vertical flight. Captain Henry Haselton believed my ideas were so good that he personally asked the Pentagon to cut me new orders for helicopter school at Pensacola. Within a few weeks, his request was granted.

During my last nine months as BAMR at the Norfolk Naval Air Station, Helen became pregnant and our first child, Jeffrey, was born. When my Pensacola orders came through, I decided to send Helen home to Franklin to stay with her mother while I completed my two months of comprehensive helicopter training. Over those two months, I learned to fly four different types of helicopters, including the tandem rotor Piasecki helicopter, which I had helped to design while a flight test engineer prior to being called back to active duty.

While at Pensacola, I continued to upgrade a few of my designs and started to build my concept of the "Glidemobile" from balsa wood. After about three weeks, I had constructed a small electric-powered vehicle designed to hover just off the floor with a series of louvers to direct its control. With the help of a few friends, I cleared the B.O.Q. dining room to give me enough space to control the flight of this strange new vehicle.

During my employment days at Piasecki, I had participated in many flight tests when the pilot and I hovered a few feet above the ground. During these tests, it became apparent that the closer we flew to the ground in a hovering state, the power setting was less than when we hovered around seventy-five feet. I had reasoned that hovering that close to the ground caused a phenomenon known as "ground effect," which meant that the helicopter blast of air into and close to the ground caused air pressure to build up with such a force that this pressure would help hold the helicopter airborne with less power required.

Applying this principal to my small balsa wood Glidemobile and surrounding the lower body of the vehicle with a tube-like balloon, air pressure built up beneath the body, which caused the model to lift free from the floor. The balloon around the bottom of the model assisted greatly in trapping the air generated by the internal propeller. This trapped air pressure seemed to lift the model from the floor uniformly. With the help of two of my

Aerial Jeep, structure prototype model.

Near-fatal helicopter crash at the Naval Air Station at Lakehurst, New Jersey, 1954.

Pensacola pilot friends, we were able to fly the Glidemobile all over the dining room floor with tremendous success. As far as we know, this was the first successful test of what would someday be known as the "Hovercraft."

After finishing helicopter flight school, I accepted a new set of orders to report to the Naval Air Station in Lakehurst, New Jersey, to join Squadron HUP-1. After three months at the naval base, a serious accident almost took my life. It occurred when a friend and I were ordered over to Piasecki Helicopter Corporation in Morton, Pennsylvania, to ferry back a new twin tandem rotor helicopter, sometimes referred to as the "little banana." As I knew all the guys at Piasecki, it was like old home week.

After signing the "deliver acceptance" papers, I climbed into the pilot's seat, followed by my copilot. After a brief system checkout I fired up the twin rotors and started to return to the Lakehurst Naval Station about sixty miles away. All went well for a while until my copilot and I decided to turn on a new boost-power system, which in simple terms is nothing more than what power steering is to the automobile. This system made it very easy to manipulate the controls without the need for excessive physical force to fly it.

As we approached the Lakehurst Naval landing strip at about 500 feet, we started a slow left turn around the famous blimp hanger where the German Hindenburg airship burned. The huge hanger now was the home for our squadron operations.

As we slowly started our left-hand descent on the boost-power system down to 150 feet, we decided to land without the system engaged. We thought that it was a good time to check out flying without this system and a good practice landing, having to apply uncomfortable physical forces on the controls during landing.

When we reached 100 feet in altitude, Jim, the copilot, reached over and flipped a switch that immediately disengaged the boost-power system. Within about fifteen seconds, we realized the control stick was rigidly frozen and could not be moved to begin leveling the helicopter now in a left-hand turn. As we both became momentarily frantic, Jim reached over to turn the boost-power control back on. But for whatever reason the power system would not engage.

Suddenly, we found ourselves in a steep left-hand turn in front of the blimp hanger with no ability to return to level flight. As we reached an altitude of fifty feet right above the landing spot, the helicopter continued to circle so steep that it became inevitable that we were about to crash into the ground. As the blades hit the ground, the entire helicopter rotor system broke into a thousand pieces of flying debris. We were on the ground spinning in a violent circle caused by the rotor hubs still rotating without blades. Incredibly, as we lay sideways in contact with the ground, Jim was able to retard the mixture control and killed the engine.

As the pilot, Jim was now on top of me when the crash came to a halt. Being on the lower side, I could hear gas dripping from the tank. I looked out the window. All I could see was a pool of high-octane gasoline all around the aircraft. Visualizing a sudden gas explosion, I frankly blacked out from fright. The next thing I remembered was being pulled out of the wreckage by a Marine guard, who later told me I kept saying over and over, "son of a bitch . . . son of a bitch . . ." as he dragged my ass away from the crash. Miraculously, neither of us was seriously hurt, although we both wound up in the air station naval hospital. Suddenly, it occurred to me that the same Sacred Heart medal that I grabbed during my water landing into the Pacific was still hanging from my neck.

Two days later I learned that a Piasecki mechanic had failed to put locking nuts on a couple of boost-power system pulleys, which caused the cables to jam the system. Consequently, I was exonerated from pilot error. However, to satisfy myself that it was not pilot error, my good friend, Commander Jim Manning, sent me a batch of photos taken of the crash, which included a copy of the failed boost-power system. No doubt about it. This was the closest call I ever experienced. I was really lucky to be alive.

Following a few weeks of recovery from this near tragedy, I was ready to return to the squadron flight line to make sure I had completely overcome the fear of flying that had developed during my recuperation. I obtained one of the HUP helicopter flight instruction manuals. Following a brief review of all the complex flight control functions, I felt confident enough to climb into another Piasecki HUP helicopter for my first flight since the accident. After a brief warmup of the engine, I made up my mind to lift off the helicopter pad. I gradually regained my confidence. I knew the accident was truly the result of a mechanical malfunction and not a pilot error.

With positive thoughts in mind, I settled down and became more comfortable with the task of flying the helicopter. With this successful flight behind me, the commanding officer called me in to ask if I felt ready to go up the coast to intercept an aircraft carrier departing Quonset Point, Rhode Island. I was also scheduled to serve as a helicopter reserve guard for a fighter group doing jet landing training. This sounded like another golden opportunity. I eagerly accepted the assignment.

One of the helicopter mechanics assigned to go with me (a guy named Harding) was from the small town of Ogdensburg, a few miles from my hometown of Franklin. After getting our new assignment, Harding and I packed all of our survival gear and supplies for a two-week trip and filed a flight plan up to Floyd Bennett field.

As we flew over the Garden State high above the traffic, we found that visibility was rapidly diminishing. By the time we reached Staten Island and the point where we had decided to cross over to land at Floyd Bennett Field, visibility approached near zero. Expressing some concern over the weather, Harding pointed out an area that was a cemetery. Picking one of the paths through the cemetery, we slowly set the chopper down before deciding what to do next. The last thing we ever thought was the possibility of parking in a cemetery overnight because of the heavy fog. The whole idea was haunting. Nevertheless, that was exactly what we planned to do. Better to be safe than sorry.

Shortly after setting down on a road located between numerous tombstones, a couple of dozen kids came out of the housing development near the boundary of the cemetery. Harding and I had all we could do to keep the kids away from the spinning helicopter blades to avoid any danger to them. With all of this excitement in a deserted cemetery on a foggy day, a police car soon arrived to help us control the children. One of the officers suggested that we try to navigate to Miller Field, a nearby army base. He thought that we could take off again, and they would lead us to Miller Field with their red lights flashing. It sounded like a good idea. Lifting off the cemetery path, we flew just above the police car, making a series of right and left turns until Miller Field finally came into view. Thanking the cops for their help after our landing, Harding and I checked into the base for the evening — after a day of unscheduled thrills. The commanding officer at Miller Air Base was kind enough to get us a good hot meal and sleeping quarters for the evening. The following morning we awoke early and refueled for our final leg off the Coast of Long Island, about fifty miles out to sea where, if all went well, we would intercept our aircraft carrier steaming down from Rhode Island.

The following morning, the fog dissipated around 9:30. After getting all the information regarding the location of the aircraft carrier, we continued our flight to the tip of Long Island. Approaching the area, we picked up the signal of the carrier's location about sixty-five miles off the coast and headed out to sea. The impressive carrier came into view loaded with Grumman jet Tiger Cats. For the next six days we took off each morning and hovered a few feet off the fantail, watching these fearless carrier pilots improve their takeoff and landing skills. Only one pilot missed a "catching wire" across the carrier's flight deck while landing and went over the side into the sea's heavy swells. Realizing the need for an urgent rescue, our helicopter flew over the downed pilot, and we went into our rescue operation. Within minutes, Harding had a soaking airman hooked to the sling and was hoisted straight up into the helicopter. This one event made the entire assignment worthwhile. I recalled my own rescue after being shot down in the Pacific. At that time there were no helicopters to pluck you out of the ocean.

After a tiring but mostly routine job of hovering over the carrier's fantail waiting for such a mishap, we finally bid farewell and departed for our uneventful return to Lakehurst.

Following my return, I received word that I would receive another assignment aboard an experimental ship in the Atlantic Ocean to do exploratory work in the Antarctica with the famed Admiral Byrd aboard. Helen now became concerned and, for the first time, thought it was about time I requested an orderly discharge back to civilian life. My first son Jeffrey was almost a year old, and needed the companionship of a father at that early age. After Helen and I talked this transfer over, we mutually agreed that I request discharge from active duty. After about one month, I got my wish and accepted my honorable discharge for the second time. I traveled home to Lake Mohawk for terminal leave and a return to civilian life. I began to dream again of starting a new aircraft company and to seek needed venture capital.

13

Returning to
Civilian Life Again

*T*he day finally came when I accepted my discharge from the
Navy for the second time. That queasy feeling you get when
your whole career is about to change before your eyes is not a
pleasant sensation. Inevitably, I made my way to the Personnel
Office where my discharge papers were waiting. There, in my termination jacket, was a Letter of Commendation from the Admiral, who was Chief of Naval Operations, citing me for the
excellent work I had accomplished over the past four years serving as the Bureau of Aeronautics Maintenance Representative
(Eastern District). Looking back now, this was one of the most
satisfying jobs a naval officer could ever hope to have.

As I shook the hands of dozens of my helicopter squadron
friends at the Naval Air Station at Lakehurst, New Jersey, I began
to realize what a vast and broad-based education I had acquired
working in a major position directly for the U.S. Navy Bureau of
Aeronautics. Four years of comprehensive World War II fighter
pilot training, flying a variety of sophisticated military aircraft,
coupled with an aeronautical engineering background left me
with the feeling that I really was ready to take on the world.

My first and most important interest was to try to be another
Piasecki, the founder of Piasecki Helicopter, the firm I worked for
prior to departing for Naval Reserve duty in 1951. During those
four years, I had the opportunity to meet key chief executive

The X-15 rocket powered aircraft, rocket engine, built by
Reaction Motors, achieved a speed of 4,093 mph at
354,108 feet. L to R: Capt. R. A. Rushworth (USAF),
J. B. McKay (NASA), Lt. Cdr. F. S. Peterson (USN),
Joe A. Walker (NASA), Neil Armstrong (NASA),
Maj. R. M. White (USAF).

officers of several of the leading aircraft companies in the United States. This, along with knowing and working with many of the top military officials running the Pentagon and the Bureau of Aeronautics, encouraged me to believe that my time had come to try to find some rich daddy who would want to back me in the development of a new and exciting concept for achieving a vertical flight aircraft. With all of the experience and contacts behind me and several of my former Piasecki Helicopter friends interested in joining me, I approached a number of wealthy individuals who could assist me in raising venture capital to carry out this work.

With this as a major objective, I returned home again, with limited severance pay, to think seriously about my future. After about two months of pursuing several of my financial hopefuls supporting my ambitious project but with no money deposited in the bank yet, I realized I needed to get a job to support a young son and my wife. Helen was well aware of my closely held ambitions of owning my own aeronautical company, so when things began to unravel, she always stood behind me. Many evenings Helen would type invention specifications until the silent hours of the morning in preparation for filing my patent applications.

On one bright morning, I decided to visit Reaction Motors in Denville, only twelve miles from home. I had worked briefly for the company before being recalled into active duty in 1951. It was about this time (1954-1955) when the rocket industry was beginning to emerge, and an effort was underway to develop and fly an aircraft to the fringes of outer space. As BAMR Representative for the Navy, I had earlier opportunities to visit Reaction Motors during my naval assignment with the rank of Lt. Commander.

Fortuitously, the personnel officer I knew in 1950 was still there. Following a brief welcome conversation, he immediately reinstated me as a Project Engineer. I was assigned to the development of the X-15 rocket powered aircraft engine. This was the engine that superseded the famous X-1 aircraft that penetrated the sound barrier. The X-15 engine was to be much more powerful

Fletcher donates rocket engines to the New Jersey Aviation Hall of Fame, used on the lunar landing and the helicopter "rocket on rotor," developed at Reaction Motors, Denville, New Jersey.

Charles J. Fletcher, Project Engineer, Reaction Motors Inc.,
being presented with "Rocket on Rotor" Award from the US Navy
Office of Naval Research. (Left) Mr. H. H. Gearinger, Supervisor
Attorney; (Right) Capt. George W. Robillard, USN Chief of Patents.

with design thrust upward of 25,000 pounds. Such force was intended to propel the X-15 aircraft to the fringes of outer space, somewhere about 100 miles high.

For the next four years, I worked diligently with several other high-powered system engineers to perfect a rocket motor that was totally new. This rocket motor, like no other, was designed to have a throttle much like a car or airplane. This gave the pilot the ability to increase acceleration from 25 percent power to maximum thrust, a feat never before accomplished. Although I played a significant role in the X-15 rocket engine development by contributing to many of its systems, too complex and perhaps too boring to mention here, I still maintained an urge to design and patent a variety of vertical lift aircraft concepts.

My dream of someday owning my own aircraft company still remained fresh in my mind. Even while at Reaction Motors, I had maintained contact with several of my former engineering friends at Piasecki Helicopter who encouraged me to consider seeking out a government contract to develop one of my several vertical lift aircraft patents. While at the Bureau of Aeronautics, I had become close friends with several high-level admirals and captains who had taken a strong personal interest in my aircraft concepts.

While still working for Reaction Motors in 1957, I decided to form my own company to continue the promotion of my patents. This company was incorporated in New Jersey in 1957 and was named Fletch-Aire. One of my ideas involved a rocket flare that could be shot up over Army troops in combat, then at peak altitude, metallic rotor blades would inflate from the hot rocket gases and allow the flare to autorotate slowly to the ground.

This unique idea interested certain munition experts at nearby Picatinny Arsenal for possible contract development. As a result, Management pulled me out of the System Engineering Group and gave me a position with Special Systems assigned to the Aerospace Marketing Team. From that time on, until I decided to run my Fletch-Aire company full time in early 1962, I spent an

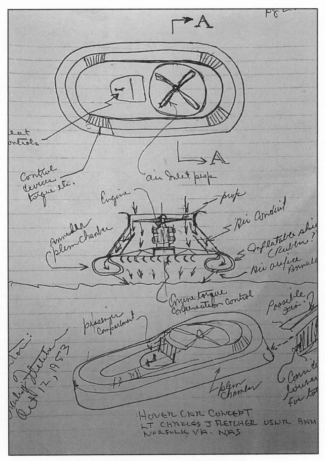

First sketch of the now-famous Hovercraft, 1953.

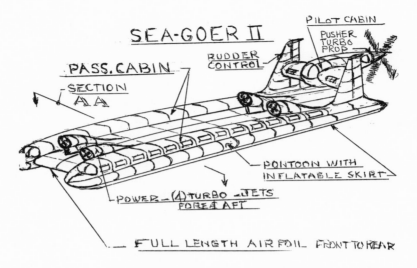

SEA-GOER II

PILOT CABIN

PUSHER TURBO PROP

PASS. CABIN

RUDDER CONTROL

SECTION A A

PONTOON WITH INFLATABLE SKIRT

POWER - (4) TURBO - JETS FORE & AFT

FULL LENGTH AIR FOIL FRONT TO REAR

SPECIFICATION

PROPELLER DIAMETER	50 IN.
HEIGHT OVERALL	40 IN.
WIDTH	66 IN.
LENGTH	171 IN.
WEIGHT EMPTY	287 LBS
DESIGN GROSS WEIGHT	482 LBS
MAX. RECOMMENDED H.P.	140 H.P.

GLIDE PERFORMANCE AT DESIGN GROSS WEIGHT

CEILING WITH 72 HP	3-6 IN.
VELOCITY FORWARD (MAX.)	40 M.P.H.

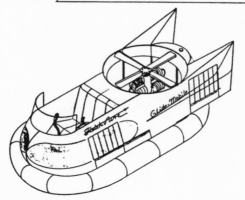

THREE-QUARTER FRONT PERSPECTIVE

Hovercraft sketch, 1958.

average of three days a week traveling in and out of Washington, D.C., attempting to convince Navy contractors to fund a variety of high-tech Reaction Motors proposals for development. It was during this period from 1957 to 1960 that I had the opportunity to meet again with the many admirals and captains holding high-level positions with the Navy and Office of Research to further my ambitions of advancing Fletch-Aire.

In late 1957, several of my friends at Reaction Motors quietly decided to join me while still employed with Reaction Motors. After several highly confidential meetings, we decided to approach a friend, Ted Pringos, to help us find some new investors to build what we referred to as a "Glidemobile." Ted was a successful restaurant owner who thought the idea was great and quickly contacted several of his friends in the hotel and restaurant business to meet at the Waldmere Hotel in Newton, our county seat. On a Sunday afternoon, I, with a group of my supporting engineering friends, gave a lecture on this visionary aeronautical vehicle, the Glidemobile.

Never had I found such an enthusiastic group of guys who wanted to see this project through to development. Within two hours, we had investment pledges of $26,000. The pledges were made with the understanding that I and the rest of the group would work on this project part-time in the evenings and on weekends. Soon I began designing the full-scale Glidemobile, about the size of a Cadillac. The Glidemobile was our version of what later became known as the now-famous "Hovercraft."

We started building the full-scale prototype in my two-car garage. The project began with a design much like the small model I built in Pensacola in 1953. Having to work with limited tools, several hours were spent learning to weld aluminum tubing with a conventional welding torch. Several people told me this was impossible to do until I met a mechanic at Reaction Motors who told me a secret about handling the torch and using a special welding rod. After weeks of practice, I became proficient in making beautiful welded joints in thin-wall aluminum tubing, a task that was supposed to be impossible.

Within four months the fuselage of the Glidemobile was reaching completion. Over the next two months, a louver control system was designed and developed to allow me to control the craft in every direction possible. I could theoretically control the craft to go forward, sideways, backwards, or rotate into right or left turns, a task that stretched the imagination to achieve by even a seasoned fighter pilot.

A 75-horsepower drone engine was located in Texas, and a special propeller was purchased from Texas to complete the power system. One last thing remained undone and that was to find a simple way to trap the air beneath the vehicle to develop the necessary pressure on the bottom of the Glidemobile in order to achieve a free flying condition. A search began to find a rubber skirt much like the Pensacola model.

After considerable deliberation, I was able to find a six-man Air Force raft that had almost the exact profile to attach to the perimeter of the Glidemobile. Cutting out the center, we were able to attach the raft to the lower frame, making it possible to trap the air internally after assembly to the covered frame. It couldn't have been a better fit for the purpose intended. This was the first inflatable skirt ever created for a Hovercraft, except for the model built in Pensacola in 1953, a model that later proved to be the final innovation that made the Hovercraft the success it is today.

Our small, enthusiastic team covered the frame with aircraft fabric. This gave us a completed Glidemobile ready for its initial testing.

What began as a "secret project" somehow had been communicated to certain military interests. We heard from my admiral friends at the Bureau of Aeronautics that the Glidemobile "secret" was leaked by some Army personnel at Fort Eustis, Virginia. We realized it wouldn't be long until a major aircraft company would make efforts to start development. About this same time, we learned that Curtiss Wright in Caldwell, New Jersey, was building a similar machine. Knowing clearly that we were up against time, we rounded up our group one Saturday morning in

First successful flight demonstration for editor of *Design News*. Victor W. Wigotsky.

late 1959 to make our first test flight at the Aeroflex Airport in nearby Andover.

It wasn't long before word reached our potential stockholders that the first test flight was about to take place. It was the first Sunday after Thanksgiving in 1959. Our small group of six part-time engineers lifted the Glidemobile onto a small flatbed truck for our trip over to Aeroflex Airport. When we arrived, there were over 150 people waiting for us from all over the Newton-Andover-Sparta area, wanting to witness our historic flight.

That particular day was laced with an abundance of sunshine but unusually high winds with gusts upward of 20 mph. We knew this condition was marginal for testing an unknown flying machine. But we were ready to go, regardless of the weather conditions. We unloaded the Glidemobile while I prepared to put on my protective fighter pilot helmet, which I had retained from the Navy. After several attempts, we hand-pulled the propeller through until the engine started to idle. Within minutes, I climbed into the front seat. Clearing everyone away, I opened the throttle, which caused the Glidemobile to lift free from the runway. With the control stick pressed forward, the Glidemobile began a trip down the runway. As I approached the runway end at about 25 mph, I quickly pulled the control stick back, which reversed the thrust and slowed down the vehicle. At the same time, I kicked in the right rudder pedal to cause the thrust to start a 360-degree turn for my trip back up the runway. Although the engine noise was loud, I could hear the claps and cheering of all those who were watching.

While all this was going on, my cousin, Gordon Bishop, at the time a columnist and special writer for the *North Jersey Herald-News,* began writing several pages of notes and taking a few black and white pictures with his camera for his now pioneering article on the success of the first Glidemobile flight. Except for the excessive winds, which caused difficult control problems, the initial flight day was a complete success. However, it was apparent that there was still work to be done to improve the louver control system and provide a better way to control the engine torque, which continually tried to turn the Glidemobile around the axis of the propeller in the opposite direction.

As we headed back to Sparta, Hardy Kircher, an MIT graduate aeronautical engineer and my friend, told me he had photographed the event on 16mm film. We were glad he recorded this now historic test because, as far as we knew, this was the first time a Hovercraft had ever flown with the inflatable skirt to contain the pressure. After reviewing the film, it became apparent that I had to add more louver control panels to acquire a faster control response, and something had to be done to control the torque that was causing me to fly with full right rudder to maintain a straight flight pattern.

About a week later, I received a call from the technical editor of *Design News*. He told me that he had heard about our flight test and would like to make arrangements to photograph the Glidemobile while it was flying on a nearby frozen lake. He told me that there were two other companies making prototypes at the request of the United States Government and that after watching tests, they were prepared to put the best design (in their opinion) on the cover of the *Design News* issue scheduled for May of 1960.

For the next two weeks, I worked feverishly in my garage half the nights and designed the system changes during the days while I traveled back and forth between Reaction Motors and Washington, D.C. After weeks of splitting my time between Reaction Motors and the evolving Glidemobile, I was ready to call the editor of *Design News* in New York to tell him that I thought we were ready to try again.

While speaking with him, he told me they were going to watch a demonstration of the Curtiss Wright model on Saturday and invited me down to Caldwell to witness the flight. I asked him how he expected me to compete against the Curtiss Wright machine when they built their machine with government research funds, reportedly of $800,000, and I had only spent around $17,000 from friends who had become Fletch-Aire stockholders. Regardless, I told the editor I would be glad to meet him in Parsippany, a small town near Curtiss Wright, to watch this demonstration.

When I arrived there, Curtiss Wright had this slick looking vehicle ready to demonstrate to the news media and, of course, my invitational sponsor from *Design News*. I began to wonder why I would ever try to compete against such a prestigious company as Curtiss Wright with all their technical resources and loads of money. Well, it was too late at that point. I had to see the demonstration results.

As the pilot climbed into the Curtiss Wright craft, he waved to the crowd and started the engines. This craft was designed to fly over water. As the craft left the shore of the lake, it flew for about seventy-five yards when all of a sudden the engine quit and the machine settled into the water. Within five to ten seconds, the tail end started to sink and the pilot began to abandon the cockpit and started to swim while the rest of the machine completely sank. About twenty minutes were used to explain to the media what may have happened. Obviously, this demonstration was a major failure and an embarrassment to Curtiss Wright.

Victor W. Wigotsky, the writer for *Design News*, said, "I told you so. You never know what will happen in these demonstrations." He then said, "Let's set up a meeting in Sparta next Saturday. I'll give you a call to give you instructions for meeting you there. I assume you will have your Glidemobile hovercraft ready to demonstrate." "Okay," I said. Nothing ventured, nothing gained.

The following Thursday evening Wigotsky called me at the house on Cherry Tree Lane where the Glidemobile had been built. He asked me if I was ready. "Well, I hope so," I replied. A few friends of mine and I worked until the twilight hours of the morning installing antitorque vanes and increased louvers to enhance control. I really believed we had our problems licked.

"Okay," Victor said, "I will see you Saturday at 10 a.m. Have your friend, Hardy Kircher, bring his 16mm camera. Maybe we can record a little bit of history."

D-Day arrived. It was the day to demonstrate our Glidemobile to the world of aeronautics as represented by *Design News*. I was up at the crack of dawn. Because of all this excitement, I just

Charles J. Fletcher, inventor of the Hovercraft, poses by a bench at Beiser's Pond in Sparta, which commemorates the first "test flight" of the craft on the pond.

couldn't sleep. By 7 a.m. I went out to the garage where the Glidemobile was and took the protective cover off from over the airframe. What a beautiful sight! Covered with aircraft canvas and spray painted in a pretty green and white design, it gave one the impression that this machine had been built by a first-class aircraft company with lots of money. In retrospect, it was our vigilant effort to keep our Fletch-Aire Company in complete secrecy, particularly regarding our employer Reaction Motors Inc., that encouraged Vic Adams and me to continue raising small sums of money from several of our engineering associate friends who intended to join Fletch-Aire if success continued.

About 8:30 a.m. Hardy showed up with his 16mm camera, soon followed by Victor Adams who took a lot of interest in the project. At about 10:15 a.m., Mr. Wigotsky showed up from *Design News*. With the help of a few neighbors and our small team of engineers, we moved the machine down a short road to a place called Beiser's Pond, which at the time was frozen over with solid ice.

Because the Glidemobile had no starter, it was necessary to start the engine by pulling the prop through by hand. After several carburetor adjustments, the engine started and we were ready to go.

Mr. Wigotsky said, "I want you to run through a series of maneuvers I have selected. If you can demonstrate that, I promise you this story will be the cover story in the next issue of *Design News* and maybe capture the attention of the aircraft industry."

With those encouraging words, I climbed into the cockpit with the engine roaring away. With the instructions that Mr. Wigotsky gave me, I slowly opened the throttle and, lo and behold, the Glidemobile raised off the ice about six to eight inches and began to drift away. Quickly moving the control stick and foot louvers to control the Glidemobile motion, I was surprised to learn I had the ability to do whatever I decided to do. After a few short runs up and down the frozen pond at about twenty-five miles per hour, I coasted back up to the shoreline where Hardy Kircher, Vic Adams, and Wigotsky were standing. Now began the real test.

Wigotsky's instructions were, "Turn left on a spot for two turns. Stop, then make two turns right and stop. Now back up for 50 feet. Stop, then move straightforward for 50 feet. Now go sideways for 50 feet. Stop, then return back sideways 50 feet from where you started."

All the time I was putting the Glidemobile through its paces, Hardy Kircher was busy taking his pictures as evidence of this historic event. Much to my surprise, every maneuver went exactly as planned.

In the meantime, some forty to fifty people had gathered on the side of the lake wondering what was going on. As I shut the Glidemobile down, a thunderous clapping of hands came from people I didn't know.

Then Wigotsky, the one-man judge and jury, said, "I was really impressed with the outstanding control demonstration you gave me. Of the other three machines I have witnessed, this has got to be the absolute best. I will be going back to New York to my office and will call you in a few days after talking to my editor. I have to tell you that I liked what I saw."

With a sigh of relief, we hauled the Glidemobile back to the garage. Frankly, I was completely exhausted from the experience. Hardy Kircher said, "I think Wigotsky was satisfied with the demo and, as for me, you did one hell of a job!"

After this test flight there seemed to be nothing left to accomplish. The Army froze my patent and claimed they had no extra funds for development. On the other hand, I kept wondering how Curtiss Wright got their contract. I figured out it had to be politics. After all, Curtiss had the bucks and the reputation.

With this big demonstration event behind me, coming home from work at Reaction Motors wasn't the same anymore. After dinner, I had always looked forward to going to the garage to work on the Glidemobile. Now that the machine had demonstrated well for *Design News*, there was little left but to sit back evenings and watch television.

About a week later, I arrived home from Reaction Motors one evening and found a letter from *Design News*. Just knowing this letter had the outcome of our previous test, I couldn't get the envelope opened fast enough. When I did, the letter from the editor read: "Congratulations on your Glidemobile demonstration. We plan to place this story in our May 1960 issue, and you will be featured in color flying the Glidemobile on the front cover."

I was overwhelmed with enthusiasm. Racing to the telephone, I called both Hardy Kircher and Victor Adams, my two closest associates and friends who had helped make this event as successful as it was.

Then it dawned on me that these magazines were widely distributed among the engineers and sales personnel at Reaction Motors. I wondered what they would say to me when my story reached the newsstands. They would now learn I had formed my own company and maybe learn that I was seeking a contract from the Army. Although I was worried to death, I no longer had control over the situation.

About two weeks later, the May issue reached Reaction Motors. There I was all over the cover in this beautiful Glidemobile just the way it was during the *Design News* demonstration. Within an hour, every engineer in the X-15 rocket engine section approached me with questions. I knew it would be only a matter of time before management would call me in to explain the details of my development and my relationship to the Fletch-Aire Company I had started. Everywhere I went, I would see a copy of *Design News* lying on the desks. In one way, the prestige of achieving a cover story was great, but on the other hand, I began to worry about the security of my job as a project engineer.

By this time I was deeply engaged in aerospace marketing, so a good part of the week I was flying into Washington, D.C., to maintain good public relations with the Navy or the Bureau of Aeronautics. After all, this was where most of the Reaction Motors aerospace contracts were coming from.

It didn't take the Navy long to recognize me as the guy on the cover of *Design News* and as a result, I became close to a lot of high-level brass who encouraged me to start operating Fletch-Aire on a full-time basis. They told me to continue pursuing a

Robert Loebelson, Director-Editor of *Aero Digest;* consultant and vertical lift aircraft concept advisor; author of John F. Kennedy speech, Dulles International Airport, Washington, D.C.

development contract with the Bureau of Ships, which had a strong interest in the Hovercraft for military assault missions. As a result, I talked Captain George Robiliard (Chief of the Office of Naval Research for Patents), Retired Rear Admiral Sands (formerly with the Bureau of Ships), General Jess Larson (formerly founder of the General Services Administration during the Truman Administration), and Robert Loebelson (editor of *Aero Digest*) into joining Fletch-Aire as directors of the company.

At last, my dream of being an aeronautical design engineer, inventor, and entrepreneur began to materialize. I was thirty-six years old and finally prepared for the challenge.

14

Back Into Business

*O*ne day, feeling the guilt of serving both Reaction Motors and my own personal interests, I talked about the problem with my wife and finally made the decision to leave Reaction Motors to run Fletch-Aire full time.

About the same time, I met Paul Gley, a fellow designer who was an illustrator for Curtiss Wright. Paul approached me about joining Fletch-Aire, and I realized I could never be successful without having additional help. Besides, Paul had this crazy idea about building a motor speed control that could be used with power drills and other woodworking equipment. Paul said he had an electronic circuit that would slow the speed of the bit of a hand drill without reducing the powerful torque to do the work. This idea was interesting because Fletch-Aire had only a few thousand dollars left from its initial group of stockholders and having a new product to sell starting out fresh seemed like a great opportunity for our fledgling firm.

Within a few weeks, Paul and I decided to set up a small office in Wayne, a growing suburb in Passaic County next to our home base of Sussex County. This would make our travel time to work about equal because Paul lived a considerable distance from my home in Sparta. Because we didn't have much working capital, I asked the landlord if he would take stock in the company in lieu of rent. He seemed quite interested in our ideas, and the drawings of our Hovercraft prepared for the military really grabbed his interest. After about a week, the landlord approached me and said he would take 50 percent of the rent in Fletch-Aire stock and 50 percent in cash in exchange for rent the first year. It was an arrangement I couldn't refuse. We gratefully accepted the offer to conserve our cash, which was then less than $6,000.

After about a month of working 12-to-14 hour days, Paul designed an electronic circuit for our new speed control, which we named "Power Plus." This was an important breakthrough because if this speed control failed to perform, we literally would have nothing to sell and in all likelihood would have to start looking for new jobs to support our families.

Paul then built a prototype model that we were ready to test. To find out how well it worked, Paul plugged the unit into an electric outlet and a small light glowed brightly, indicating it was receiving the power.

Plugging a half-horsepower drill into the "Power Plus," Paul put his new invention to the test: drilling a one-inch hole through a piece of steel. To accomplish this, it was necessary to turn our power knob down to the lowest possible drill speed to prevent the drill from overheating.

Paul and I had no doubt that the drill would operate. The real question was, could the "Power Plus" slow the drill speed down to a crawl without losing the force necessary to keep the drill from stalling?

Understanding what we were trying to accomplish, Paul fastened the steel bar in the bench vise and started to drill. We both agreed that if this drill cut smoothly into the steel bar with a full one-inch hole without burning the "Power Plus" out, we would really have something great.

As Paul applied pressure on the drill to begin cutting the hole, it was obvious that the drill maintained constant rotational speed all the time Paul was applying pressure to the metal bar. Much to our amazement, the metal began spiraling out with ease. This first test of our product was passed with flying colors!

I told Paul that before we could start marketing the "Power Plus," we had to be sure that we could repeat this event at least thirty times in succession to be certain the electronic SCRs (silicone control rectifiers) could take the heat for an extended period of time. Over the next two days, we drilled again and again with no failures occurring.

After spending another week determining where we would market and package the product, Paul and I decided to design a fancy red box for the product and immediately ordered components to build 1,000 units.

In the meantime, we hired a friend of mine, Joe Murphy, to hit the road traveling up through New England visiting all known hardware stores. We had decided that this was where all the power tools were being sold, so it was good logic that men purchasing these tools would welcome a new speed control.

Like a timely lifesaver, Joe came in every Monday morning with several orders. These stores liked what they saw, and Joe's demonstration sold the product. Within sixty days, the cash started streaming in from the "Power Plus" sales.

Magazines placed free ads in the new product introduction section and this, too, started to bring in several inquiries from commercial companies. Things started to move along swiftly. We were flying high, without wings! The first cash paid all our bills, and the balance of funds began giving us an income to live on.

While all this was happening, I was still sending technical reports to the U.S. Army, hoping to get development funds for continued research of the Glidemobile. However, after several highly successful months, a series of unexpected events occurred that almost ruined the business.

For some unknown reason, Paul began to act strange. He took on an egotistical air with his colleagues and was often rude. He was losing interest in the company. Then one morning he came to work and declared that he never should have given the "Power Plus" speed control to Fletch-Aire, and that he was going to sell back his stock to me and go off on his own.

Because of his unexplained behavior, I suspected something was about to happen and it did. For a moment I didn't know what to do. Finally, I said to Paul, "If this is the way you feel about it, I'll pay you $2,000 for your Fletch-Aire shares and give you a total release, except the "Power Plus" stays.

The following day, Paul sold his stock to me and the initial shock set in. Not being extremely versed in electronics, I had to act quickly to save this growing business. After placing an ad in the local Wayne newspaper, I was fortunate to hire an electronics engineer who turned out to be a great guy — and a lifesaver. Within a month, production had resumed and everything was turning around.

Paul was gone, and I still found it difficult to understand how his personality could have changed so fast. While our new electronics engineer was building speed controls, I was still communicating with the Department of Research at Fort Eustis, Virginia.

One morning, I got a call from one of the Fort Eustis project engineers who told me they decided to place my Glidemobile proposal into a secrecy classification status that would prohibit me from gaining a patent on the Glidemobile concept, which from a technical point of view later became known as the "Hovercraft." They did tell me, however, that because of their interest, they would consider a further development contract with their next year's fiscal budget approval.

Realizing that the next year's budget was still seven months away, my engineer and I decided we had better find an electronics company that could produce the "Power Plus" speed controls at a faster rate so we could spend more time on marketing to increase sales.

After making inquiries, a friend told me about a small electronics subcontractor who could probably help with our production. The company my friend had in mind was Whippany Electronics located in nearby Fairfield, next to Wayne.

Calling the company, I talked to its President, John Padalino, who set up a meeting to evaluate our product. After spending about an hour with John it was decided that Whippany Electronics would manufacture the speed control provided I would give him an order for 500 units at a time. John, being the clever guy he was with electronic innovations, actually improved the product.

Over the next two months, a few things happened to change the course of my interest in becoming an entrepreneur. We soon learned that General Electric was copying our "Power Plus" idea. We had never filed for a patent, and General Electric manufactured the critical SCR part that was the heart of the product. With their enormous capital resources, General Electric cut the price from our $29.95 to $19.95, and overnight our sales plummeted. To conserve cash, I reluctantly had to let Jim, my project engineer, go to pay Whippany Electronics for the new speed controls being made.

With activities slowing down, I was sitting in the office one evening reading *The Wall Street Journal* section, "The Mart," an advertising section promoting various business opportunities, such as properties for sale, companies for sale, and a host of other things. Scanning the ads, I read one that said, "Large English Tudor home with 735 acres located in the town of Upper Jay, New York, just twelve miles from Lake Placid." At the bottom of the ad were these words: "Will sell or trade," with the telephone number.

Getting a little desperate for working capital due to shrinking sales, I figured I'd give him a call to see what it was all about. Dialing the number, a guy answered by the name of Alexander Kueller, who quickly discussed the property and asked what I had to offer. Telling him all I had was a small research company with lots of ideas for building a new type of flying vehicle and other unique products, he took an interest in what I was telling him about Fletch-Aire. He seemed to be particularly interested in our Glidemobile project.

Mr. Kueller said to me, "The Glidemobile sounds like a great idea for getting around in the Everglades in Florida." Evidently, Al, as he asked me to call him, believed that this was exactly the vehicle we needed to get around the wetlands and swamps to reach fishing areas not accessible by the typical boat.

Before hanging up, Al said that although he had around 125 inquiries about his property, he asked if he could stop by if I had the time after 7 p.m. the following evening. I was overwhelmed with his interest and invited him over.

After hanging up I thought, "Why would an intelligent guy who owned a huge estate with a million dollar building want to consider stock in such a small, start-up company like Fletch-Aire?" By this time it was getting late, but I just sat there wondering if there was a chance in hell that Al would make such a risky deal.

It must have been around 9 p.m. when I got to thinking about my good friend, Ted Pringos, who had helped raise the funds to develop the Glidemobile and the beginning of Fletch-Aire. Ted, who was a devoted Greek Orthodox Catholic, had at one time given me a skinny beeswax candle and said, "Charlie, if you ever get down and out, which you probably will, simply light this candle and turn off the lights and meditate about your problem and ask God for some help." Feeling despondent, I had nothing to lose, so I lit the beeswax candle and sat silently in that dark office in Wayne, just hoping and praying that Al Kueller, the guy I was to meet the following day, would somehow see enough good in what Fletch-Aire was trying to accomplish to say, "Let's make a deal." As this skinny beeswax candle started to burn down safely in the tray, I decided to pick up my dilapidated briefcase and head for home.

15

Seize the Opportunity

*T*hose were the words our 1940 Franklin High School graduation class chose as our motto. To this day, those words have
always left a strong impression on me whenever a potential
opportunity arises.

Al Kueller was such an opportunity.

Driving to work the following morning, I couldn't help
thinking: "What if the office building burned down because of
that beeswax candle?" No one had phoned me at my home in
Sparta, so I thought everything would be all right when I arrived.
But a burning candle seemed like a dumb thing to do.

Arriving at my office in Wayne, it was obvious that the
building was still standing. When I opened the door to my office,
there was the beeswax candle melted down like a glob of caramel
taffy. The room was permeated with the smell of sweet wax. All
through the day I kept thinking, "What's the chance of Al Kueller
never showing up for our late 7 p.m. meeting?"

To create a little interest, I had three quite large 2'x 4' technical illustrations of the "Hovercraft of the Future," which Paul
Gley designed to perfection in color from my patent designs. Paul
possessed a marvelous gift for bringing new products to life.
These machines were designed to carry 150 passengers over the
water at speeds upwards of 70 mph. Although these drawings
made it appear as if the Hovercraft of tomorrow was ready to fly

off the wall, I had no idea that thirty years later, the vehicle would indeed be flying over the English Channel or the Army and Navy would have Hovercrafts capable of carrying three huge tanks with thirty Marines designed for beachhead invasions. But that is exactly what happened by early 1992.

Late in the afternoon, those negative thoughts began popping into my head again. "What if Al didn't show up?" Sales of speed controls were slowing down because General Electric jumped in with their own design to undercut the "Power Plus" Speed Control. I kept reminding myself that I no longer had my assistant engineer, Jim, to help me. Here I was with only my part-time secretary, Irene, who was acting as a receptionist, typing my letters, and doing all the miscellaneous things a secretary would do to keep an office humming.

It was around 5:30 p.m., after Irene had left for the day, the telephone rang. My first thought was that Al was calling to say he couldn't make our meeting. Somehow, I couldn't get those negative thoughts out of my head. As I picked up the phone, I immediately recognized Al's voice. "I called to say I will be a few minutes late. See you soon."

At exactly 7:20 p.m. Al drove up in his new Lincoln Town Car. I had been watching for him from my office, which was located up a flight of stairs on the second floor. As Al came through the door, there seemed to be a bit of magic to our mutual personalities. Al was a tall man, well dressed in a casual sport coat. His handshake was firm and sincere.

First he walked around our engineering room where all of Paul Gley's eye-catching color illustrations were hanging on a wall. I briefly explained a bit of my history as a former naval fighter pilot who became serious about designing vertical lift aircraft for the military after graduating from the Academy of Aeronautics. When I showed him the cover story printed in *Design News*, he seemed to get excited over the idea that these machines would some day replace the airboats used in the Everglades of Florida.

After forty-five minutes of get-acquainted conversation, Al told me about his fabulous 738-acre estate in the heart of the

Adirondacks located twelve miles from Lake Placid and, more importantly, only four miles from New York State's multi-million dollar ski resort, White Face Mountain. During our conversation, Al explained that the lodge had been built by a wealthy Chicago lawyer around 1902 and who married a local girl from the nearby Wells family. Al said he named the place "Wellscroft Lodge." Wellscroft cost well over $2 million at that time and included a local library for the town of Upper Jay in honor of his bride. This place was an immense, well-built structure using local hardwood. It had fourteen bedrooms, a master bedroom, a large dining room, a billiard room designed specifically for that game, a bar, and servants' quarters. The third floor was capable of sleeping thirty guests. There was a caretaker's house and a stable to bed six horses with an apartment for the horse barn keeper on a second floor where a 1,000 pound fire bell hung from a tower.

Al continued to say that he had, as a builder, picked up the estate in the early 1950s when it had been in liquidation. As the story goes, a lawyer from Chicago had been wiped out in the stock market crash in 1929 and the place had been going downhill until Al bought it for less than it cost to build. Being a builder with two sons working for him, Al quickly refurbished all the rooms, roof, and outbuildings to almost their original conditions and then spent many weekends there for several years following his purchase.

Always curious, I asked Al why he wanted to sell such a beautiful estate, and he was quick to tell me that he was just plain tired of traveling the 480 miles every weekend for so many years. His construction business was expanding with jobs in the Caribbean Islands, making less time to really enjoy Wellscroft.

After two hours of revealing and fascinating conversation, Al said, "You know, I probably am crazy and my wife will confirm I must be nuts, but I must tell you there is something about what you are doing that would refresh my interest if there was some way we could make a deal." Al obviously didn't need the money from the sale. Even if I wanted to find a way to buy it, I couldn't raise that kind of capital anyway.

Al came right to the point. "I like your ambition to try and build this so-called Hovercraft, and you seem like a guy who will do all he can to see such a project to completion. Although I have at least another 125 offers that would give a large part of the deal to me in cash, I really don't need the cash. First, you never saw this place called Wellscroft Lodge, except for these pictures I'm showing you. So I'll tell you what I will do. You and your wife Helen take a ride up to Upper Jay. I'll tell Armon, the French caretaker, you are coming for the weekend. Look over the property and come back and give me a call and we will talk further."

For a moment, I couldn't believe what I was hearing. Anyway, suppose he would sell. Where the hell would I get that kind of money? I had all I could do to finance my company as it was. Before Al left, we shook hands. As he did, I felt a sincere hand that somehow removed the depressed feeling I had from all our start-up problems.

That weekend in the middle of July 1963, Helen and I set out on this adventure to Wellscroft. Some five hours later, we approached the property in the quaint little country town of Upper Jay, a public recreation area. A guy who owned property a mile from Wellscroft's entrance operated a small Disneyland type park called "The Land of Make-Believe." As I learned later, the owner had worked for several years with Walt Disney and had retired with this miniature Disney Park idea.

As we passed through the large stone-gated entrance, we drove up a winding road along the mountain to the reception parking area behind a huge lodge. The pine trees were 80 to 100 feet high and the view across the valley was breathtaking. In answer to my knock on the door, the caretaker appeared. He evidently had been expecting us because he knew our names and invited us to look around.

This place was just too much for me to put into words. Solid oak throughout, several large fireplaces on the first and second floors, exquisitely decorated bedrooms designed by Al's wife, as I later learned from Armon. Most of the windows were stained glass, as well as numerous light fixtures that spiraled all through

Wellscroft Lodge

the building. At the far end was a quaint bar with every liquor label imaginable, exhibiting a stuffed deer head overlooking the bar. The deer head was both eye-catching and eerie, as if it were still alive and staring right at you.

Armon took us up to the master bedroom, with walk-in closets almost as large as my bathroom at home. The bathroom was equipped with large French-style basins, reminiscent of fixtures you would see in movies of the early 1900s.

Helen, standing in disbelief at the lodge, finally spoke up and said, "What a joint!" We settled in and rested for an hour before Armon called us down for dinner. In the main dining room, under a colorful Tiffany lamp, Armon had the table lit with candles and the lights turned low. After sitting down, Armon appeared with shish kebab, which he quickly doused with brandy and then lit into a flaming torch. Helen kicked me under the table in her subtle way and whispered, "Now this is living."

After touring the property for most of Saturday and Sunday morning, we departed for home in utter disbelief. All the way back, we asked each other how we could ever manage this lodge and still run a start-up business? We didn't even know what Al had in mind if we agreed we were interested.

On Tuesday of that week, Al called my office and asked me what I had thought. Frankly, I was speechless, but before we hung up I had agreed to meet him again the following evening to talk further. The whole next day I kept wondering, "What if Al was willing to negotiate. Money was out of the question." Cash was getting low and business was starting to decline with powerful GE as my new competitor.

Tuesday evening Al arrived on schedule and came in with his projector and numerous color slides of the renovation work he and his wife had done during the refurbishing process. Al insisted that I look at them. After the slide show, he said, "If you really think you can handle Wellscroft, I'll make a deal with you. You give me a note for $20,000 and stock in Fletch-Aire at $5 per share for a total of $75,000 and I will transfer the property over to your company.

What a deal! This was a "no cash" proposition payable with only 5 percent of Fletch-Aire's almost worthless stock. How could I resist? The asset value alone would boost my balance sheet, providing me with collateral for a continued business loan. Al continued with his presentation: "Look, if I bring my attorney in on this deal, he will argue against it and the deal will be off. So, you go home and draft up some kind of acquisition paper for me to read structured around the Fletch-Aire stock arrangement. If I think it's okay, you bring your lawyer and meet me in my lawyer's office, and we will tell the attorneys to butt out and let us close the sale."

On the way home that evening from my office in Wayne, I kept asking myself, "What the hell am I getting myself into? What's the hitch to this deal?" I had always heard that if a deal sounded too good, watch out — something was wrong.

The following day I consulted an acquisition book I had in my pile of textbooks and began writing a legal acquisition agreement based on our agreed terms. With little or no legal experience except for my brief knowledge of U.S. patent law, I completed what I thought was a decent draft of our mutual understanding. After completing the document, my wife typed it. Frankly, double-spaced, it looked pretty impressive.

The next day I called an attorney, Frank Bright, whom I had known as a kid. Frank was one of the guys who had tied me to a tree and set me afire before I was saved by my neighbor. Still, Frank was a sharp lawyer. I explained the deal to Frank who immediately told me I was nuts to write this document myself. I told Frank that this was the way Al had wanted it so I had done it. I informed Frank that Al wanted to meet next Saturday in his lawyer's office for the closing and all Frank had to do was read the agreement, sit back quietly with Al's attorney, and let us sign a closing. Frank couldn't believe what I was saying but agreed to read what I had developed for an agreement and promised to go to the closing.

Saturday afternoon came. After picking up Frank, we departed for Hasbrouck Heights next to Teterboro Airport, only

minutes from New York City where Al's lawyer was located. On
the way to Hasbrouck Heights, which was about a 40-mile trip
from Sparta, Frank read over my proposed agreement. About
halfway there, he acknowledged with total disbelief that my document was satisfactory. "If this is what Al wants to do, this
agreement isn't bad for you," Frank said.

I smiled proudly. "It ought to be good for me. I wrote it."

Frank asked me how I had written the text of the agreement
so well without any legal experience. I told him how I had
referred to an acquisition book with a sample document and tried
to follow the format using our agreed settlement terms.

Frank was dumbfounded. "There's no doubt that if Al signs
this abortion of an agreement, it will be legal. However, Al's got
to be out of his mind. He is literally handing over to you a million
dollar asset for stock he could paper his wall with, at least until
this business of yours grows."

Turning off Route 46 into Hasbrouck Heights, we made a
few more turns onto some side streets and finally found the
offices of Al's lawyer. As Al planned, we walked in, introduced
ourselves, and discussed the content of my self-made closing
agreement. Al's lawyer asked to see a copy. Taking about five
minutes to read it through, I carefully observed his facial expres-
sions, which varied considerably while he was reading to himself.
His face was stern, then he would shake his head back and forth
as to appear in total disbelief, then he would glance at Al as if to
say, "Are you nuts?" without uttering a word. Al's lawyer finally
said, "If it were my deal, I'd throw this document into the can.
However, if this is what you want, Al, what can I say?" Al looked
his lawyer right in the eyes and said: "It may not be for you, but,
yes, this is the way I discussed it with Charlie and this is what I
want to do." With that, Al declared, "Okay, if Charlie has nothing
to add with his attorney, you guys go over there at the other table
and chat while Charlie and I wrap up this agreement."

Within no more than three minutes, Al and I signed the
papers I had prepared, after which Al asked both lawyers to witness the event.

Frank spoke up while signing the contract as a witness, saying, "I've been a lawyer for better than sixteen years and in all my life I have never had the pleasure of participating in such an unbelievable closing. But if this is what makes you guys happy, God bless you both."

Turning to Al I said, "Congratulations, Al. Welcome to Fletch-Aire, Inc. As one of our illustrious directors, let's hope for both of us, that you didn't make a mistake."

On the way home, Frank said he never saw a company our size go from rags to riches so fast. "Just what the hell are you going to do with this place now that you own it?" At that moment I was so delighted about the whole deal that I was completely speechless.

As I was driving back to my house after dropping Frank off, I couldn't help but wonder what Helen would think. As I walked into the house, Helen greeted me at the door and said, "Tell me, Al wasn't crazy enough to sign your agreement, right? I can tell by the look on your face."

"Here, look at the papers. Al did the deal!"

"I can't believe what I'm seeing," Helen said. "How are we ever going to run this place and still try to cope with the business in Wayne?"

With tears of joy in my eyes I told Helen, "Where there's a will, there's a way. We will just do it."

For the next two weeks, I concentrated solely on the activities of Fletch-Aire, that is getting the speed control orders shipped and adjusting to the fact that Fletch-Aire was now the new owner of the Wellscroft Lodge.

As expected, Al called me and said that he thought it would be a good idea to take a trip back up to Wellscroft the next Saturday so we could explain to Armon, the caretaker, that I was going to be his new boss. I agreed with Al. If I was going to take control of Wellscroft, I'd better go there with him to decide on a managerial path to take.

Before we left, I thought it would be a great idea to rent a friend's airplane, which he kept at Morristown Airport, and offered to fly Al up to Lake Placid. So when I called him and suggested the idea of renting a plane, he thought this would be a great change from his usually boring trip by car.

Al McWilliams, a good friend and President of McWilliams Forge Company, was one of the guys who had bought stock in Fletch-Aire at about the same time that Ted Pringos, my restaurant pal, encouraged me to sell stock in the Hovercraft project several months prior. Al's company owned a plane at Morristown Airport, so I asked him if I could rent it to fly up to Lake Placid. McWilliams, who knew of my background of flying off carriers for the U.S. Navy, didn't even hesitate when I asked. He said, "Go ahead. Just pay for the fuel and the plane is yours."

Al Kueller and I agreed to meet at the Morristown Airport the following Friday. Al was brimming with excitement over our pending trip by plane. Around 10 a.m. that Friday, Al and I climbed into McWilliams's Cessna 172 and departed for Wellscroft in the Adirondacks Mountains. Never having flown there before and especially in a light plane, I was hoping the weather over Lake Placid would be clear.

The trip started by following the New York Turnpike over Albany, then on to Port Henry, where we refueled the aircraft before heading northwest deep into the 7,500-foot mountains of the Adirondacks. Before taking off over Port Henry, I climbed up to 10,500 feet to be sure we had plenty of altitude above the mountains to minimize the strong, gusty mountain currents that could make flying severely bumpy and perhaps even dangerous.

After fifteen minutes over the mountains, it sure enough was as rough as riding a steer at the Dallas rodeo. I told Al to keep his eyes open for Lake Placid because the airport was located at the south end of town. This beautiful crystal clear deep blue lake came into view and, within minutes, we spotted and landed at the Lake Placid Airport.

We rented a car and drove down the valley to Wellscroft, about twelve miles away. Driving over to the Lodge, I asked Al what Armon did that paid for the operation of the Lodge restaurant. It seemed to me that the night Helen and I stayed at

Wellscroft there weren't enough dinner guests to pay the light bill much less the taxes and operating overhead.

For the first time, Al confessed that Wellscroft needed new management and suggested that Armon, who was a great chef, had to go. He admitted to losing control of expenses and was, in fact, subsidizing Armon's operation.

After settling into our beautiful bedroom, Al and I made the rounds the next two days traveling around the area. I met many of Al's closest friends, and he explained to them how I was taking over the lodge. We had a great evening in Lake Placid watching ice-skaters performing at the Olympic Arena.

Sunday morning came and Al and I agreed that we would have to advise Armon that he was fired because we were closing the lodge down for minor repairs. This was no easy task since Armon believed that this was going to be his permanent place to do as he pleased. When we told him that his services were no longer needed, we could see fire in his eyes and resentment in being forced to leave. Al and I agreed to give him two weeks to get his things together so he could make some plans as to where he would go. Flying back to Morristown that Sunday afternoon, Al and I discussed Armon's attitude over his dismissal. We both felt Armon might do something terrible to the property before he left.

Placing the problem aside for the moment, I decided to let Al fly the plane as we approached New York City from about 100 miles out. Al had a real sense of feel and quickly enjoyed hanging onto the controls. Within minutes I had Al making slow gradual turns and climbing and descending to get a total feeling of what flying by the seat of your pants was all about.

As we approached the north side of New York, I realized that our fuel was getting dangerously low, so I reduced our power and limped west over to Morristown on a shortcut path to avoid a serious problem of an emergency landing. Fortunately, we landed without incident. Before Al and I went our separate ways, he told me that the thrill of flying there and back and the way I handled myself with Armon had convinced him that he had made a good deal, and that he was happy to be part of Fletch-Aire as an active member of the Board of Directors.

Getting back to work on Monday, I knew I had to act immediately to get a new manager. I placed an ad in the Plattsburgh newspaper for a chef, from which I received three replies. I picked one person for an interview and headed back to Wellscroft by car the following Friday.

As I drove to the lodge, I began to realize why Al Kueller was tired of the long and tedious trip every weekend. Yet this was a golden opportunity to make my company grow with the Wellscroft equity free and clear of any mortgage.

Arriving at the lodge, I found a note saying that Armon had gone to Albany for the weekend. The following morning, the person who had contacted me for an interview showed up with his family: wife, eighteen-year-old daughter, and two boys, ages eight and twelve. After talking briefly to Eric, a Swedish immigrant, I learned he had an extensive background in the restaurant management field. I also realized that his family could be a tremendous help by working in the lodge with so many rooms to clean and care for. Due to a lack of time, I decided to hire him. He told me that his wife could handle the cooking and the kids would help clean up around the lodge and provide the wood for the lodge's six distinct fireplaces. His daughter was quite pretty and was an ideal candidate for tending bar. For $100 per week and free lodging, I had another great deal and hired them on the spot.

Within a matter of a few weeks, Eric and his family seemed to settle in nicely. To help them with transportation at this remote lodge at the top of a mountain, I bought a used station wagon that Eric and his wife, Elsa, used to shop for food and supplies at nearby Lake Placid.

During one of my early weekend visits, Eric pulled me aside to tell me something I did not know about Armon. Eric told me that one Friday evening shortly after Armon departed, six beautiful Canadian girls from Montreal had showed up at the front desk and asked where their rooms were. Much to Eric's surprise,

Armon had been in business with these girls, selling their sweet little bodies to the Air Force guys stationed at Plattsburgh, New York.

After Eric told me this, I recalled my first visit to the lodge. We were curious as how Armon covered the overhead with what seemed to be so little traffic. Evidently, the call girl business had been flourishing without Al Kueller's knowledge. It took Eric about two months before local residents got the word the call girl business had ended, and the lodge was a great place to wine, dine, and stay.

As the winter season approached, Eric suggested that we advertise at the White Face Mountain Ski Lodge by putting up a handmade sign featuring a small band who had contacted him looking for work. Getting desperate for cash flow, Eric hired the band. That Saturday night after the sign had been hung at White Face, lo and behold, the parking lot quickly filled with cars. Fortunately, Elsa had anticipated some increase in dinner traffic and had prepared a smorgasbord with all the trimmings. The band was so popular with Beatles-style music that the place became swamped with the ski crowd from White Face Mountain. Eric was so excited that he had Elsa make up a new sign for White Face that read "Featuring at Wellscroft — The Adirondack Beatles." In a few weeks the lodge was booked to capacity every week from Thursday to Monday and the bar tended by Eric's daughter was really raking in the cash.

For the next two months, Helen and I and our son, Jeffrey, left New Jersey every Friday around 2 p.m. to drive the long, tedious trip to Wellscroft. Come Sunday evenings, Helen would add up the cash, pay all the bills, leave Eric enough for the following week's food and booze, and then depart for the long trip back to Jersey.

Business at the lodge became so good that we always managed to bring back between $1,200 and $1,400, which helped pay our mortgage and subsidize our main efforts of developing our new company, Aerosystems, the result of a name change in 1962.

February rolled around and we began to realize that the ski season would come to a halt shortly after the snowfall ended in March. As predicted, by the beginning of April business had dropped off sharply, and cash receipts barely covered expenses.

I remember one late Saturday night when I was sitting at the bar with two guys to my right and a third guy, half in the bag, perched to my left. I said something like: "I wish one of you guys had a good idea to help this joint make some money." With that said, the drunk at the end of the bar turned his head and said, "Did you ever look out back?" You've got three miles of timber on this property that's worth a fortune. Why don't you cut some timber?"

Not knowing anything about the timber business, the following morning I grabbed the telephone book and checked the yellow pages for someone in the timber business. The name "Ward Lumber" popped up in the display ads. Rather than call, I decided to visit them since they were only two miles up the road from the lodge.

After a fifteen-minute discussion with one of the Ward brothers, I detected a sincere interest on their part to walk the property to determine what type of contract could be developed. The following morning two of their top lumberjacks arrived at Wellscroft and made their survey.

Shortly after noon, they asked me to consider a proposal whereby they would agree to cut every fourth tree that was a minimum of 24 inches in diameter with them limiting their cutting to no more that 33 acres. They explained to me that they would pay me based on board feet cut, but I never really knew what that would mean in dollars and cents.

Since I was eager to generate a little cash at a time things were getting financially tight, I signed a contract. Before I left for New Jersey, a lawyer friend, Daniel Manning, suggested that I hire one of the local kids in the area to count the number of logs on each truck, including measuring each log's diameter. That sounded like a good idea. How in the hell would I ever know how much they were taking out if I didn't do that? So with Mr.

Manning's help, we hired a kid for $4 an hour. Since there was only one road out, the kid could just sit there and keep track of the log cutting.

The first week I returned to Wellscroft after log cutting had started. Ward Lumber had a check waiting for me in the amount of $1,700. At that time, this was big bucks for the company, and I knew they were just beginning their tree-cutting program. As I returned each Friday night over the next two months, checks became larger and larger until I had accumulated $72,000. That was almost as much as I had paid Mr. Kueller for the property in Aerosystems stock. Since I had this cash, I thought it would be a good idea if I paid Mr. Kueller the $20,000 one-year note early. This way he would realize I did right by taking over the property, and he would have greater confidence in me.

In the summer of '65, I decided a cash sale of the entire Wellscroft property would provide me with a real financial start to cover our own growth plans. Also, these funds would lend further credibility with my bank and would perhaps extend financing further should a small technology company seek out an interest in consolidation as a stepping-stone to a public offering. Following my intuition, I ran a small ad in the Mart section of *The Wall Street Journal* similar to the ad that had attracted me in the early part of '64. I received around a dozen responses of which I screened out and pursued three. One was from the owners of nearby Camelback Ski Resort, a stone's throw from our executive offices in North Jersey. Camelback was located in the nearby Poconos where the ski slopes were ideal to meet the demand of the young crowd out of New York.

After exchanging a variety of company documents, their president, Fred Frankel, requested talks to establish a basic interest in a deal.

After several weeks of negotiation, we decided to take $30,000 up front with a promissory note for $250,000 payable over two years and still retain a 33 percent interest in the project. At the outset, things went fairly well; however, a little over a year, the payments on the note began to slip. After several legal proceedings, we took the lodge back with all its furnishings together with fifteen acres of surrounding property.

The initial $30,000 from the original sale of Wellscroft was subsequently used in the acquisition of Serin Enterprises, a harrowing event in my life, one that again taught me harsh lessons about being a full-fledged entrepreneur.

16

A Brief Relationship
with Robert Vesco

*O*ne of the most fascinating people I ever knew was Robert Vesco, the New Jersey entrepreneur whom the media made into a celebrity "fugitive" when he, according to the U.S. Justice Department, fled from the United States with some $225 million of stockholders' money he had stashed away in secret bank accounts around the world. After wandering around the globe, hiding from authorities, Vesco reportedly lives in Cuba today under "house arrest," according to the media.

My encounter with Vesco happened when I was planning to leave my position at Reaction Motors in Denville, not far from my home in Sparta. My last job with Reaction Motors involved the procurement of new development contracts relating to rocket propulsion concepts.

After three years of working as an Applications Engineer, designing new and exotic rocket systems for the U.S. Navy and Air Force, my job required me to prepare technical proposals translating these ideas and concepts into plain English in hopes I could encourage the military to fund these projects for development. To accomplish this I had to plan a trip each week to visit some military procurement group in the Bureau of Aeronautics in Washington, D.C., or Edwards Air Force Base in California. At these meetings I stood at a podium and addressed several high-ranking admirals or generals or whoever took an interest in my proposed concept. As an Applications Engineer, I had developed the ability to attract upward of $75 million in new studies. That was the backbone of new money to continue financial support for Reaction Motors.

I was engaged in the marketing of advanced rocket-powered systems while continuing to complete final development of the X-15 rocket, a system designed to fly the X-15 aircraft at speeds of 4,000 miles per hour and 100 miles high to the fringe of outer space. This was the rocket system I had worked on from late 1955 through 1959 while assigned to the Systems Engineering Group headed by Arthur Brukardt. Ironically, it was Art Brukardt who became Vice President of my company, Technology General, after Reaction Motors' parent company, Thiokol, decided to move the liquid rocket engine firm to Salt Lake City, home of the solid rocket boosters used on NASA's spacecraft.

During this time, I began to see the downfall of Reaction Motors. The X-15 rocket tests near Denville were cracking many foundations because of the high-powered thrust that rattled everything for five miles around. Residents were filing numerous lawsuits to repair their cracked windows and foundations.

It was less than two years since I had built the Glidemobile prototype (Hovercraft) while still working full-time for Reaction Motors. It had become apparent that the British Company, Hovercraft Ltd., was testing their first Hovercraft, as reported in *Aviation Week* magazine. That vehicle somehow looked like an enlarged copy of my own Glidemobile. Little did I know that it was built from my own design that I had sent the U.S. Army and Development Command at Fort Eustis, Virginia, two-and-a-half years earlier. It wasn't evident until the litigation between British Hovercraft Ltd. and the U.S. Justice Department in the early 1980s that the British design was a copy of the Fletch-Aire Company's Glidemobile.

During the litigation, a Justice Department attorney, Mr. Townsend, learned that after my proposal was terminated for a lack of development funds, a technical engineer at Fort Eustis passed on my concept to a friend in Canada, who in turn sold the concept to an engineer in England. Shortly after, British Hover-craft Ltd. was financed by the British Government, and the Hovercraft was built around a design concept exactly like my Army proposal.

Not realizing the enormous significance of the British proj-ect and its history at the time, I continued the pursuit of my own start-up business with other ideas and developments already dis-cussed. None of my own interests had anything to do directly with my brief relationship with Robert Vesco, who, in his corporate dealings in the early 1970s, became the world's "Most Wanted" international thief.

My association with Vesco began around 1965 shortly after I had acquired my first company, then known as Serin Enterprises (later renamed Metaltec Corporation). I was still working with my associate, Paul Gley, out of my small office in Wayne. I was mak-ing brief visits to my former boss at Reaction Motors, Al Menden-hall. Like myself, Al left Reaction Motors with several engineers to start a new company called Astro Systems International. Al was a dynamic, handsome man who had been crippled by polio early in life. His charismatic personality and drive got his company off the ground. A public bond financing led to several military con-tracts, placing Astro Systems in a well-established position in the aerospace industry.

Because of my personal admiration for Al Mendenhall and his brilliant marketing ability, I would often slip by Astro Systems to see how well he was doing. At that time he had a secretary who became a good friend because she also had worked at Reaction Motors. Because I did not have the facilities that Astro Systems had to prepare technical proposals, I would often stop by their offices to solicit help from her for typing out and printing various proposals. At that time Al was a close friend of Robert Vesco, who was then operating a small company doing a half-million dollars in sales. Astro Systems was located around the corner from Vesco's office. Al had learned of the success I was having with my new hand-tool control "Power Plus" and wanted me to show this product to Vesco. Several meetings were set up with Vesco to discuss his interest in acquiring the rights to my product. For several weeks, my wife and I would go to dinner with Al and Vesco. That was the beginning of a one-on-one relationship. During our meetings, I observed that Vesco had an eye-piercing ability to convince you that he would acquire anything he decided to go after. His aggressiveness was persistent in getting whatever he wanted.

As we sat at the table and continued to negotiate, Vesco became ever more aggressive, sometimes insulting and even bordering on threatening us. Somehow I was always able to see through him and resist his increasing pressure to acquire my speed control patent. On other occasions, mostly during our social activities, Vesco would mellow and become extremely pleasant. He possessed the ability to completely change his personality to fit any situation.

During this period, when Astro Systems International was led by Al Mendenhall, I found myself becoming somewhat envious of their early rapid success in selling a major underwriter bond issue for $1.5 million. My weekly visits to Astro Systems allowed me to maintain a close relationship with Al and his wife, Barbara. Al was always impressed with his close friend Robert Vesco. Al would include Helen and me in many weekend dinner engagements where Vesco and his wife were always present. After about four months of an ongoing relationship with Al and Robert, I began to learn of Vesco's many trips to the Caribbean. Just what his activities were down there I never quite figured out until one day I learned Vesco was running out of cash. A few days later I received a short note from Vesco, asking me if I would introduce him to my good friend at the Iron Bank, Charlie French. Vesco wanted to borrow $200,000 from the bank. After receiving the note, I called Vesco and told him I would introduce him to French's loan officer, Roger Rice. I told Vesco I could not assure him they would be able to assist him financially. A few days later I happened to be in the Iron Bank in Morristown and told Roger of Vesco's request. Not really sure of Vesco's business beyond the small local company he ran, I informed Roger that Vesco seemed to make numerous trips to the Bahamas, but I never learned just what the Caribbean trips were for.

"Roger," I said, "Vesco wants to borrow $200,000. Be careful until you can learn more about his business structure before honoring his request."

A few weeks later, Roger called to tell me that he had talked with Vesco and agreed to loan him half of the $200,000 he was requesting. He also said Vesco was working with a group of international financiers at the Butler Bank in the Bahamas, putting together some kind of deal to buy a California public company.

About three weeks went by when Al Mendenhall called to tell me what he had learned from his secretary, who seemed to have daily contact with Vesco. Al was upset with her because she became involved with Vesco on a day-to-day basis. This relationship worried Al, who suspected Vesco was up to no good. Then, one evening while sitting around after dinner, his secretary told Al, "I have decided to work for Vesco."

Al was speechless. She was an exceptional secretary who probably knew more about the day-to-day details of Astro Systems operations than Al did himself. The shocking news devastated Al and immediately strained his relationship with Vesco. She called Al the following day because she felt badly about what was happening. In her conversation with Al, the secretary revealed that Vesco had made a deal with IOS, an international investment company run by Bernie Cornfield, a controversial money manager, to borrow $17 million to buy out a California firm, Electronic Specialties Co. ESC was doing some $40 million a year in sales. This was the biggest deal Vesco had ever made. Suddenly, Vesco's International Controls Corporation became a giant overnight with more that 3,000 employees.

Once Vesco acquired Electronic Specialty, I read in the media that he was successful in acquiring a company every other week or so. Al Mendenhall called me one day to say that Vesco had just purchased Caldwell Airport in Essex County, New Jersey. Next it was several small technical firms in the Fairfield area, including Radiation Machinery.

Vesco's industrial growth seemed to be skyrocketing, while I was just completing my own strategy to launch a new public company through the sale of a small issue for Aerosystems Technology. I had just acquired Eclipse Systems and Whippany Electronics, both in Fairfield. The acquisition of these companies thrust Aerosystems on a growth curve from $850,000 to $3 million in sales in less than seven months. I also became interested in Datron Systems, a new computer company manufacturing a piece of hardware that was building sales. Again, through Al Mendenhall, I had met the president of Datron Systems and was able to get my former boss at Reaction Motors, Art Brukardt, a job with the company. Not long after Art began to work with Datron he called to tell me the company was beginning to experience cash flow problems and thought Aerosystems Technology could acquire the company. I contacted Datron to discuss our interest in a possible acquisition. I recall that a guy named Jack was the company's president. As our negotiations began, I learned that Vesco was also making his bid for acquiring Datron Systems. After a month of serious negotiations, it became apparent that Vesco's sudden flow of cash from his connections in the Bahamas greatly exceeded my expectations, since I was dealing primarily with stock-for-stock, whereas Vesco was dealing with cash. Vesco's $350,000 in cash handily won the acquisition fight for Datron. Vesco was the winner. I was the loser, for the moment. Vesco was infuriated when he found out I was competing with him. From that time on, I had no further business or social relationship with him.

About four months after Vesco acquired Datron Systems, Al called again and told me Datron was filing Chapter XI and that Vesco lost his full investment. At the time, I couldn't have been happier to know that he was the real loser.

Two years passed and Vesco became engaged in the IOS deal, the big international investment company that had lent Vesco the funds to buy Electronic Specialty. Soon after, IOS itself came under severe financial trouble. Somehow, Vesco was able to infiltrate the management of IOS with a small investment of $7 million while effecting a cancellation of his $17 million with IOS as part of his acquisition price to take control of the company. Word got around that Vesco became chairman of IOS, terminated Bernie Cornfield, the president, and took complete financial control of IOS.

Over the next several months, Vesco sold for cash most of IOS's stock holdings reported to be in excess of $224 million and fled to Costa Rica with his wife, family, and Al Mendenhall's former secretary.

For the next several years, this secretary became Vesco's right arm and secretary of International Controls. The media then made Vesco a celebrity, crowning him as the largest international thief of the century. With the embezzled $224 million, he set up headquarters in Costa Rica, established his own army, smuggling guns and ammunition. He allegedly became heavily engaged in trafficking drugs.

Finally, the scandal broke when U.S. Attorney General George Mitchell and others were indicted over a reported $200,000 cash contribution from Vesco to President Richard Nixon. Included in the indictments were our glamorous, efficient corporate secretary of the past. Following her indictment, her deposition of the Vesco affair led to her being fired by Vesco in the Bahamas.

Because of her testimony that fingered Vesco, the U.S. Justice Department finally exonerated her in exchange for the Vesco information she willingly provided.

In 1980, I received a call from her. For more than thirty minutes she unraveled the Vesco story and suggested she stop by to see me. Arriving at my office at Technology General a few days later, she sat down with me behind closed doors and briefly told me the whole story, which we recorded on tape. For some reason she contacted me because she knew I wrote many technical proposals while at Reaction Motors, and she believed I would be the one person who could write of her experience of her long personal relationship with Vesco as his private secretary and member of the board.

Because of her persistence, I decided to take on the challenge. Over a two-month period, she would come to my office around 3 o'clock each afternoon and, with a voice recorder, would tell me her complete story, revealing much more information about Robert Vesco's activities than was ever published in the media. For the next six months, I transcribed her daily notes describing his various alleged illicit activities into what I thought could be a best-seller.

I eventually reached the point when I felt I had a sufficient manuscript to submit to a publisher who agreed to review the story. For whatever reason, three days after the manuscript was sent to the publisher, our former secretary called and said it was urgent that she and her husband see me at once.

At my office, she informed me that she had received a phone threat, warning, "if this Vesco story is published, you will be history." The voice on the phone said "We will take care of you in our own way." She was so frightened that she and her new husband would be killed, that any book on Vesco, even a best-seller, was not worth the risk. The Vesco manuscript remains with me, unpublished to this day.

17

Confronting Serpents

I had heard through my network of contacts about an up-and-coming company in my hometown of Franklin. The company had developed a way of manufacturing writing instrument components owned by Andrew Serin. I knew of Serin going back a few years. He may have had some business problems, according to one of my local banking friends. This was about the time ten or fifteen small pen companies were starting up, primarily on the New Jersey side of the Hudson River opposite the New York City area where making pens was a strong industry. It was one of the early exoduses of manufacturing from New York's high-rent districts to New Jersey, where the cost of business was much less in those days.

Someone told Andy Serin to contact me at my office in Wayne to discuss financing for his company. I knew I had a few bucks left over from the Wellscroft timber contract, so I agreed to meet him at my office. When Andy arrived, I learned he was experiencing serious financial problems and needed help fast. I decided to go back to Franklin the following day to look at his operation, which impressed me considering the volume of work he was turning out. Having heard several stories of the company's dealings and financial problems, I decided to take precautions.

Over the next few weeks, I studied the competition of this business very carefully and then called Serin Enterprises. After getting a pretty good idea of the production organization, I decided to call Andy back to Wayne to discuss a possible business relationship. At our meeting, Andy told me he had signed a letter of intent to sell the company to a Harvard graduate who had failed to come up with the necessary cash, so Andy wanted to cancel the agreement. I knew this would present a problem unless I could get this individual to sign off before I got involved. However, before doing so, I prepared an acquisition contract agreeing to acquire the assets of Serin Enterprises including all his customers subject to terminating the previous agreement and taking over full financial control. With that program in mind, I agreed I would give Andy 100,000 shares of Aerosystems Technology and invest $27,000 of the Wellscroft money to help the company survive.

When Andy agreed to this deal, confirming that Serin Enterprises held $550,000 in machinery and equipment and inventory with receivables estimated to be worth in excess of $425,000, I assumed that the worst thing that could happen would be getting out of the deal with at least 100 percent more than my investment.

After discussing the plan with Al Kueller, we agreed to go ahead, subject to terminating the former letter of intent. With this tentative agreement in place, I was able to locate this individual the following day by contacting the New York City Harvard Club. After speaking to him on the telephone, he agreed to meet me at the club to discuss his legal position.

At this meeting, he told me that his bank had trouble getting credit information on Serin and had recommended that he abandon his option to buy Serin Enterprises for his proposed offer of $300,000. As soon as he said that, I asked if he would be willing to cancel his option since he couldn't get the $300,000 from his bank. He replied: "Yes, I guess this exposure is more than I want. I'll release my position in favor of Aerosystems." As he was able to locate a secretary at the club, he dictated a memo terminating his option. The moment he signed off, my offer became immediately effective. On the way home from the Harvard Club, I couldn't help thinking that just maybe this gentleman's bank knew more about Serin Enterprises than I had bargained for.

Within a week, I had shut down my office in Wayne and relocated to one of the extra large offices at Serin Enterprises. After checking out the work force in detail, I decided that if I was going to be successful in turning the company around, that I'd better cut out the duplication effort and get rid of the deadwood. As a result, six jobs were cut out the following Monday. I called the remaining forty-six employees into a private session.

I used a tactic of Henry Michaels, top administrator at Reaction Motors. He would climb up on one of the plant A-frames and give his guys a pep talk that was as powerful as Roosevelt declaring war. Everybody liked Henry because he had balls and told everyone just how it was and what he expected it to be.

That's exactly the way I did it at Serin, except I climbed up on the front of a forklift, had somebody raise me to the top of the plant, and laid it on the line. There was much enthusiasm doing it this way, and the guys seemed to respond to new leadership and applauded me at the end of the pep talk. If anything, they got the message quickly. Everything we planned to do was all business. The bottom line was what it was all about.

During the first two weeks, I made a point to review Serin Enterprise's financing and banking connections. Within a week, I began to realize there were hidden liabilities that Andy had never mentioned. It was obvious the token $30,000 invested in the business was being used up much faster than I had planned. In addition to that problem, I received a notice from an Elizabeth bank that claimed Serin Enterprises had overdrawn an old payroll account by $11,500 that had never been disclosed to me prior to the purchase. For the first time I realized why the other gentleman's bank hesitated to extend credit to him to purchase Serin Enterprises.

In an effort to halt the rapid downturn, I contacted a good friend who had invested earlier in the Hovercraft project. I mentioned earlier that Al McWilliams was the president of McWilliams Forge Company in nearby Denville and the guy who let me use his plane to fly Al Kueller up to Wellscroft. Al McWilliams's brother was also a former naval aviator who flew with Fighting Squadron 20 in the Pacific, so Al and I shared many common interests.

After telling Al of my rapidly declining cash position, he suggested that we meet with Charlie French, the president of Morristown First Iron Bank. Al was a director of the bank, so it was easy to set up a meeting. Al suggested that we meet at his home on Saturday afternoon with Charlie French to discuss Serin's financial problems. During that meeting, Charlie French and I seemed to hit it off, and before I left he agreed to give me a $30,000 unsecured line of credit, which we agreed Serin needed desperately. The last thing I remember Charlie asking me was, "Do you believe I've given you enough?" Overwhelmed with the $30,000 loan, I told him I was reasonably sure that the $30,000 would handle our problems.

Over the next three weeks, a half dozen unknown snakes popped out, and before the end of the month, things were looking just as grim as ever. Our accountant discovered that the company had failed to file payroll tax returns over a period of six months. Our first clue came when an IRS agent paid us a visit to investigate why payroll tax proceeds were not being paid. Our accountant, Jack Stifelman, was called in, and he quickly found several tax reporting forms hidden deep inside a desk without a penny forwarded to the IRS. This shocking dilemma really had me worried because the audit Jack ran showed the company owed $57,000 in back payroll taxes.

By this time, Charlie French, the bank president, had $30,000 invested. I decided to call Charlie to apprise him of the critical tax situation. After contacting my good friend Alexander McWilliams again, a second meeting was arranged by the large swimming pool of the McWilliams estate. Again Charlie showed up and asked me to explain the tax problem.

Before our meeting was over, Charlie had placed a call through to a friend he knew in the tax department and set up a meeting the first thing Monday morning at his bank office. It was there that Charlie French structured a new $300,000 SBA loan guaranteed by the Iron Bank and collateralized by the machinery and equipment valued upward of $400,000. Although we all realized this loan would take another month to close, Charlie agreed to advance another $50,000 provided we fired the bookkeeper and hired a new comptroller to manage the cash flow.

With the deal made with the IRS to pay our debt over time and keep all new taxes current, we proceeded to smooth things out. The good news was that Serin's sales were brisk and receivables were building. Within a week, we had hired a new comptroller who wouldn't spend a dime without knowing he would recover 50 cents for every 10 cents spent.

Within four months, cash flow improved so rapidly that the bank accelerated the SBA closing, and the proceeds paid both the taxes and improved payable "agings," a term used to imply how old the debt is. Vendors actually began to extend credit to me primarily for the purchase of large volumes of brass and aluminum used extensively for the manufacture of writing instrument caps and barrels that made up the body of ballpoint pens.

Shortly thereafter, I suggested to Serin that it would be advantageous for my parent company, Aerosystems Technology, to take title to at least the twenty-two acres, including the plant, creating an incentive for the Small Business Administration to grant a second $300,000 loan, which we badly needed to expand our working capital.

After talking to Serin about this thought, I learned that a lawyer friend of his, D. C., held the mortgage on the plant property and was sucking out high-interest (15 percent) mortgage payments every month. As an additional bonus, Serin said he had to turn over the cash proceeds he was collecting for the scrap metal being sold, which was substantial.

Although I was still learning about the Serin business, it became evident that this unscrupulous lawyer, D. C., was taking all of the scrap metal cash payments, which represented about $2,500 per month, in addition to his regular mortgage fee. After investigating the matter more closely, Serin admitted that he had persuaded the lawyer to give him the property mortgage provided he gave him all the proceeds from the scrap metal in cash under

Jay R. Benenson, lifelong attorney and "deal maker."

the table. As it turned out, more often than not, monthly scrap metal sales for cash exceeded the monthly mortgage payment, thereby giving the lawyer 100 percent plus interest dividend on the mortgage payment. Upon learning about this, I became furious.

Here we were ready to proceed with a badly needed SBA loan when I learned of this horrible situation. More importantly, this cash was the company's equity. Because of the seriousness of the situation, we again consulted our accountant, Jack Stifelman, who recommended that I meet with a young lawyer friend of his to discuss the situation. The lawyer's name was Jay Benenson, a sharp attorney fresh out of law school. He was a handsome, young, eager guy who had joined his father-in-law's firm in Newark, New Jersey.

Jack Stifelman made the arrangements for us to meet Mr. Benenson in his Newark office where we told Jay of our pending new SBA loan application and the corrupt relationship Serin was having with his lawyer, who, in turn, owned and controlled the property being offered as collateral for the new $300,000 SBA loan. When D. C. learned that I was negotiating a deal with the Iron Bank, he began to realize that if this loan went through, he would lose his high-paying metal scrap income as a bonus for the mortgage he had given financially strapped Serin Enterprises.

Jay thought about the situation for a few minutes and then asked me to go back to the Serin plant and search the correspondence file for all documents and letters that the lawyer may have ever written.

What I found the following day was unbelievable! In one of the files, I ran across a letter from D. C. written on his legal stationary that said to Mr. Serin, "if I can pay one of the SBA loan officers $15,000 in cash, I (D. C.) will be able to get you a loan for $300,000 provided Serin Enterprises continues to pay me all monies received from the sale of scrap." Realizing this letter was good ammunition to force the lawyer to relinquish the mortgage hold he had over the company, I sent a copy to Jay. Upon receiving this letter, Jay told me that it was sufficient evidence to have him disbarred.

The following day, Jay called me into his Newark office and set up a plan to force the unscrupulous lawyer's hand. Jay said, "Charlie, I'll play the good cop, and you play the bad cop. Tell you what I want you to do. When you get back to your office, I want you to call the lawyer and tell him straight out that you have a copy of his blackmail letter to bribe the SBA, and that unless he makes a move to return $50,000 of the stolen scrap money taken over the past year, I will send a copy of the letter to the New Jersey Bar Ethics Committee, which would cause him lose his license to practice law, if not send him away for participating in a federal bribe."

Upon hearing those words, the lawyer blew his top, screaming out of control. Not being able to tolerate his verbal abuse, I hung up the telephone and called Jay to play his role of the good cop.

This is exactly what Jay did. He called the lawyer and told him that he had me as his client who could not be controlled unless Mr. C. was willing to settle the claim. Thus the roles of Good Cop and Bad Cop were beginning to show great progress.

The next day I called the lawyer again. Evidently, he had been expecting to hear from me after Jay's conversation. I started the conversation loud and shouted at him, indicating that unless the matter was settled within fifteen days, I would personally hand deliver his bribery letter to the New Jersey Bar Association. This conversation started his blood to boil because all he said was, "Screw you! I'll take this matter up with your attorney, Mr. Jay Benenson."

In the meantime, Jay and I had made a bet that we would extract at least $30,000 out of D.C.'s hide within thirty days or I would pay Jay a $1,000 bonus for his efforts. The next call D.C. made to Jay was a definite plea to restrain me from sending his letter to the Ethics Committee. Further, he would immediately agree to settle this matter out of court if we would accept $35,000 cash.

As it turned out, Jay extracted a check from the lawyer just seventeen days later, which gave us some much needed cash to expand our manufacturing operation. With Jay getting a third of

Acquisition of the Metaltec Corporation. Corporate office
and plant in Franklin, NJ.

the settlement, less his $1,000 for me winning his bet, the money we anticipated saving from scrap sales (approximately $65,000 annually) and with the net settlement proceeds of $23,000 we would be well on our way to recovery.

About two months later the SBA papers and investigation were completed, and Jay and I were called to the Iron Bank to close the deal. This was a sweetheart deal with interest down around 4.5 percent.

When we arrived, we found one shocking item incomplete. The bank did not have Mr. C's release from the mortgage, and he was refusing to allow the mortgage to be paid off unless we paid him $5,000 for doing so. The bastard was making a last ditch stand to get even with us. So after conferring with the bank's principals, Charlie French, the president, said, "Let's send a courier down to D. C.'s office in Paterson with a $5,000 Aerosystems check just as he demanded. Then we will call him to sign off on the mortgage and have the courier return the paperwork."

That is exactly what we did. When the courier arrived at D.C.'s office, he witnessed the lawyer signing off on the documents and then gave him our Aerosystems check before departing to go back to the Iron Bank. As soon as the courier arrived back, Charlie French made sure the signatures were correct and then placed a "stop payment" order on D.C.'s Aerosystems' $5,000 check.

Three days later D. C. found out a stop payment had been placed on his check and called my office in Franklin, shouting at the top of his lungs. I never heard more cuss words in one minute in my entire life! Was he pissed off! After he wound down, there was a brief pause, during which I interjected, "Sir, what goes around has finally come around. You snake! You finally got what you deserve!" With that, I hung up.

We never heard from him again. However, about a year later we read in the *Newark Star-Ledger* that he had been disbarred from practicing law in New Jersey. Evidently, one of his fraudulent deals had finally caught up with him.

After the SBA loan was closed, our Board of Directors elected me as Chairman and reappointed Andrew Serin to the job of Production Manager.

As things began to improve financially, it turned out to be a serious mistake letting the former owner, Andrew Serin, continue to manage production and monitor shipments. For about two months, sales were brisk, but for some reason, our balance sheet revealed purchases of raw materials were heavier than usual with little or no growth in daily sales. Knowing Serin's reputation, not to mention the bouncing payroll checks at the former Elizabeth bank that we had no knowledge of, and the serious payroll tax default for which the company was guilty, I became suspicious of Serin's activity to a point where I had one of our trusted foreman keep a close eye on his activities.

After two weeks, foreman Joe, my wife's brother, came to me and said, "Why does Andy Serin come in at 5 a.m. and load up his station wagon with pen components for a trip into New York City to make a delivery to our customers?" "Good question, Joe." I said. Why would a man of his responsibility want to work that hard when our regular shipments were leaving via a common carrier about 4 p.m. in the afternoon.

Joe and I immediately smelled something foul about these daily trips. We put together a plan that called for help from a state trooper friend of mine. From the way Serin was operating at such an early hour of the morning, I suspected he was loading his station wagon with large quantities of merchandise and delivering our product to one or more of his friendly accounts for cash under the table and without bills of lading or even invoicing records.

We had a meeting with a trooper who traveled Route 23 leading into New York City. He agreed to stop Serin on his way into the city around Newfoundland, New Jersey. Just as we suspected, Serin, after being pulled over, had no bills of lading or invoicing for the merchandise. Nevertheless, he had the name of the account written on the cartons with a black ink marker, a method we did use in shipping merchandise. When Serin could not provide the supporting paperwork, the trooper called me at the

Charles J. Fletcher receiving a President Nixon award
presented by Executive Secretary Beverly Jansen.

office and asked me to come down to the Newfoundland station where he had detained Serin.

When I arrived, Serin began running scared and begged to settle the problem. The trooper recorded the incident.

The following day, we held a board meeting and fired Serin and filed suit against him, demanding a recovery of all stolen merchandise. While the case was pending before the court, our board of directors agreed to change the name of the Company from Serin Enterprises to Metaltec corporation in order to establish a new corporate image. About six months later, the company was beginning to expand rapidly.

Before the trial was scheduled to start, Andy's lawyer called our attorney, Jay Benenson, for a settlement meeting. After a week of negotiation, Serin agreed to terminate $160,000 of payments off the company purchase price and transfer two adjacent homes providing rental income to the company. Included under the settlement were fourteen additional acres of land in exchange for a full release. This substantial reduction in our long-term debt, including an increase in our real estate assets, really made our financial statements look good and definitely enhanced our banking relationship with Charlie French's Iron Bank of Morristown.

It wasn't long after the close of this incident and a change of management for Metaltec that a package arrived from the White House. Inside was a picture sent to me and signed by President Richard Nixon showing Nixon signing new legislation into law using a newly designed pen I manufactured at Metaltec. The award was presented to me by Executive Secretary Beverly Jansen.

18

The Public Offering

*A*s the company progressed through the early 1960s, I became interested in exploring the possibility of public financing, reasoning that if I could acquire substantial money from the sale of stock, I could investigate the purchase of other technology companies that would accelerate both total cash flow and rapid growth. As 1967 approached, the stock market started to warm up and financial institutions began looking for sound companies that could use additional funds efficiently from the sale of stock.

At the time, I was reading *The Wall Street Journal* as if it were the Bible. One day as I turned to the section called "The Advertising Mart," I spotted a brief ad from a New York attorney who claimed to have numerous Wall Street contacts for making a stock offering. I was interested and called Bernard Jay Coven, attorney, and made arrangements to visit him at his 57th Street office in New York City.

The following day I drove into New York and took the elevator up to his office on the fourth floor. As I opened the door, there were five or six other guys sitting around a smoke-filled lobby just waiting to see Mr. Financial Fix-It. At the reception desk was a serious looking elderly lady, a cigarette hanging from her mouth, setting up meetings. I later learned that Mr. Coven was her son. Bernard Jay Coven became one of my most beloved friends. "Bernie," as his friends and associates call him, was a

Bernard Jay Coven, Esq. with his wife, Harriet.

Harvard graduate and had a lot to do with writing a substantial portion of the Securities Exchange Act of 1933.

But on that first day of introduction, Mrs. "C," as they referred to Bernie's mother, asked me to go into her son's office to discuss my financial needs.

Meeting Bernie for the first time was an experience all by itself. Sitting behind his desk strewn with books and papers from one end to the other, he asked me to describe my company and its financial needs. For whatever reason, there seemed to be a personality mix that seemed to connect. My aeronautical background and my numerous aeronautical patents related to vertical lift aircraft, together with my serious inventive interests, seemed to catch his attention.

After explaining that I had purchased the pen component business from Serin Enterprises, now known as Metaltec, as a base for researching my aeronautical interests, Bernie said he would consider doing what was called a "Regulation A" public offering, limiting the stock offering to a maximum of $300,000, which to me seemed like a lot of cash. I especially liked not having to pay it back.

Before I left his office, Bernie said he would consider doing the deal if I would advance him $5,000 to cover his initial effort and expenses. However, I was reluctant to give him $5,000 without any assurance of him completing the offering. Yet, for some reason, our meeting gave me faith in Bernie because it seemed to me that he was a hardworking attorney who impressed me working fifteen to eighteen hours a day nonstop.

Two days later, another friend, Fred Gearhart, who had flown the Hovercraft prototype, confirmed that Bernie had a fast operation for getting small public issues off the ground. Fred also had a Wall Street financial institution known as Gearhart and Ottis, but lacked the ability of completing risky underwritings, which was exactly what Aerosystems Technology Corporation was at that particular time.

After about a week, I called Bernie and told him that a check for $5,000 was on the way, and I wanted to schedule another appointment to get the deal started.

For the next four months, I left Aerosystems office three or four times a week late in the afternoon and drove to Bernie's office on 57th Street. During this time he would come to the office around 2:30 or 3 p.m. and begin his daily work screening potential companies. At the same time one of his associates, a student from New York University, would prepare the offering circular used to sell the stock with Securities and Exchange approval, if and when authorized.

While there, I began to understand Bernie's operation. His take from these issues as they were approved was 10 percent of the proceeds plus low-cost options in the company. If the stock sold out, he would make a handsome profit from the Regulation A offering.

My own workdays ran sixteen to eighteen hours a day. I'd manage Aerosystems Technology and then leave for Bernie's office where I'd spend the entire evening writing and revising our public offering prospectus, injecting new and current financial statements being prepared by our accountant, Jack Stifelman. While doing this, I'd consult with Bernie about other attractive company deals and even offered to help write the required Regulation A prospectus.

Many an evening we would leave his office around 2:30 a.m. and hike down to the Stage Door Deli, one of New York's finest. There, Bernie would order a thickly sliced liver steak covered with burnt onions with a side order of thickly sliced tomatoes. At 3:30 a.m., I would drive him all the way out to Long Island where he lived and then continue home to New Jersey where occasionally I arrived as late as 6:45 a.m. I must say that my wife was extremely understanding about those weird, long nightly events and never really expressed anger. However, she did worry about my lack of sleep and general health.

After exhausting preparatory work, Bernie finally received a letter from the Securities and Exchange Commission requesting a meeting in their New York office to discuss the content of our offering circular. At this meeting the SEC agent expressed concern that most of our revenue was derived from the pen company, yet we were promoting the development of aeronautical research concepts. Bernie quickly explained the relationship, telling the SEC agent that the pen company provided the necessary working capital to carry out our day-to-day research. When we left the New York SEC office, we did not really know what the examiner thought about Bernie's explanation.

Hoping the SEC would accept Bernie's story about Aerosystems' situation with the pen company, the following day we went down to Wall Street to talk with the young president of Mayflower Securities about doing the public offering. I recall him being a sharp-tongued young kid who impressed me as having a wise-guy type personality. After spending about an hour in his office and Bernie explaining all about Aerosystems and its objective, the young man paused for a moment and then, looking Bernie straight in the eye, said, "Tell you what I think. Take this piece of shit out of here and forget it. This offering would make a market maker throw up." With that statement, Bernie and I picked up our package of Aerosystems papers and left the Mayflower Securities office. Since it was about lunchtime, Bernie suggested we stop in a deli for a quick sandwich and discuss our strategy further. Finally, he said, "Forget about this guy, kid. His time will come and he'll be banned from the street. True enough, about six months later the SEC closed down the Mayflower Securities office for breaking SEC laws. As we continued lunch Bernie said, "I still have a good friend who's a stockbroker who just may take our deal. Just as soon as we finish lunch, I'll take you over to meet Joe Berk."

Since Bernie thought it would be a tough issue to sell to a broker, as a favor for me, we headed over to the office of Joe Berk, President of Berk Securities. After meeting with Berk, a deal was signed to sell the stock, if approved by the SEC. Two days following the Berk Securities meeting, Bernie got a call from the examiner that the SEC reluctantly approved the offering. Much to my amazement, Joe Berk and his friends in the securities business oversold the issue at $4 per share. Within two weeks, the issue rose to $9 per share and stayed there for a few months when

Aerosystems Technology Board of Directors, 1962.
Back row: Arthur Brukardt, Vice President (left);
Charles J. Fletcher, President (right).
Front row: Robert Loebelson, Editor, *Aero Digest* (left);
General Jess Larson, USAF ret. (center); and
Alexander P. Kueller, President, Kueller Project Development (right).

it gradually settled back to $4 per share and stayed there for over a year.

Shortly afterward, Bernie, Joe Berk, and I closed out the public issue and paid off all the commissions for the sale of stock. Aerosystems Technology ended up with a net $260,000 for 33 percent of the company, which was more cash than we ever had gotten debt free since the company incorporated back in 1957.

As things began to flow smoothly for Aerosystems, a friend at the Iron Bank, Roger Rice, contacted me and asked if I would be interested in purchasing a company called Eclipse Systems, a manufacturer of specialized spray-coating guns and pressure tanks, air-driven mixers, and numerous other supporting equipment used in the spray coating field. Wanting to acquire a new company, as we had planned to broaden our product lines, I told Roger that I would be interested if the bank would finance the buyout. Roger's reply was he had a brother-in-law, Jack Merrill, who was a senior vice president with Mobil Oil in New York who had learned that the owner of Eclipse Systems had lost interest in running the company and wanted to sell it. Roger then said that Jack Merrill knew a friend who was a senior investor for private placements at Value Line Securities who might be interested in taking an investment risk.

A few days later, Roger arranged a meeting with Jack Merrill, who told me if we could find Eclipse Systems of interest, he would approach Value Line to invest in Aerosystems. That would provide sufficient funds.

As an engineer and inventor, I was learning how big business really worked. Wall Street was an endless avenue of opportunities — and risks. As a Navy fighter pilot, I was conditioned to take risks, but risks that were carefully executed for the sake of my own survival, physical and now financial — a whole new exciting game!

19

Eclipse Added to
Corporate Family

*A*fter our accountant, Jack Stifelman, and I spent a few hours reviewing Eclipse's last annual financial statement, we found reason to believe Eclipse Systems could be an extremely profitable acquisition if management was replaced with new blood that had the guts to provide good leadership. Jack and I agreed this could be a great acquisition company.

I called the owner, Warren Beach, Jr., whose father was a brilliant inventor responsible for the new spray gun concept known as electrostatic spraying.

Eclipse had just developed this new spray gun designed to spray lacquers and paints by passing the material through a chamber that caused the paint to spray with a large field of static electricity. Eclipse's newly designed systems for spraying permitted the paint to take on a strong magnetic field upon discharge from the gun causing the paint spray to attract directly onto a metal object. Not only did the paint spray charge the paint with an electrostatic force, it also caused the paint spray to be attracted to the rear side of the object being painted. Thus, a revolutionary new paint system had just been developed that could save thousands of dollars by having the electrostatically charged spray attract onto both the front and rear surfaces of the object being sprayed with little or no wasted paint overspray.

I called Beach to see if I could arrange to close the deal. During our conversation, Warren told me that he had just given an option to a small research company working at the Picatinny Arsenal Reservation in Wharton, not too far from where I lived. For a moment after hearing this, I became extremely distraught. Wondering what I could do, I asked Warren if I could have an option in the event the one he had fell through. Warren then told me that the first company had fifteen days remaining on their option to buy Eclipse, and if they ran into difficulty raising the cash, he would call me. Not satisfied with that, I asked Warren to meet me in my office in Franklin to negotiate a purchase price so that if his deal stumbled, at least I would have an additional thirty days to find the necessary cash. Warren agreed that having my backup deal was better than no deal at all if his number one option fell through.

Warren came to the office the following day and within hours, I had dictated an agreement to acquire Eclipse Systems for $150,000 cash and 100,000 shares of then Aerosystems Technology Corporation stock at a price of $4 per share for a total acquisition price of $550,000. After I had negotiated this option offer with Warren, I immediately called Jack Merrill to tell him to approach his friend at Value Line.

The same week that Eclipse's number one purchase option was about to expire, Jack Merrill called me from New York and told me that if our option moved in place, Value Line was ready to make $260,000 available through a private placement at Aerosystems public offering price of $4 per share.

On Friday of that same week at 3 p.m., Warren Beach called me and told me that his first deal had fallen through because their bank would not lend them the money.

Upon learning of the good news that our option would kick in on Monday, Jack arranged a meeting with his friend who was a vice president at Value Line. At this meeting, he discussed the $150,000 cash requirement with the balance in stock. Jack's friend thought our option deal was an excellent buyout and agreed to review our financial needs. About a week went by before Jack called again and said that an agreement was being prepared for review.

I was on my way into New York City to visit Bernie Coven in my old 1968 Lincoln. You remember the model – where the rear doors open backward. As a lover of gadgets, I was sporting one of the first car phones available at the time when my new cellular phone rang. Surprised out of my wits, I answered it to hear Jack Merrill on the line. Jack quickly relayed (through an occasional blast of static) that our friend at Value Line had just called him and asked if I would stop in front of Value Line's offices at East 46th Street where the vice president's secretary would be waiting with a package for me.

Although Jack never said what the package contents were, I told him I would be there in thirty-five minutes. As I worked my way through the Lincoln Tunnel and through the congested city, I kept wondering what would be in this envelope.

As I pulled up alongside the curb at Value Line's office, there was this beautiful six-foot girl who looked like a model, standing there with a large brown envelope. As I rolled down my window to speak to her, she asked if I were Charles Fletcher. With a friendly smile, I answered "yes." After showing identification I took the package, exchanged a few more pleasant words, and drove to Bernie's office on West 57th Street.

When I arrived at the parking garage just a block away, I stepped over to the parking lot reception office to see what was inside the big brown envelope. As I pulled out this stack of papers, there attached to the first page of a legal document was a check for $269,000. Never in my wildest dreams had I expected to see a check before finalizing and reviewing a contract.

Within minutes I arrived at Bernie's office. It was now 3 p.m. His smoke-filled lobby was filled with clients anxiously waiting for a deal. By this time, I had become quite friendly with Bernie and his mother, who ran the office. Without hesitation, I strolled past his mother and entered Bernie's private office.

Bernie was always happy to see me. I handed him my Value Line envelope. His desk was loaded with numerous deals and papers waiting to be screened for acceptance of a new public offering. Upon opening my envelope, Bernie, pushing his badly worn executive chair back, said, "Wait a minute! I like the check, but let's see just what this substantial agreement says." For the next thirty minutes, Bernie leafed through page after page crossing out paragraph after paragraph with a heavy red pen. I was scared to death that he was going to kill the deal. In his usual plainspoken way Bernie said that this deal was going to be his way or no deal at all. Without blinking an eye, he picked up the telephone and called the person at Value Line who had written the cover letter. For the next forty-five minutes Bernie explained paragraph by paragraph why he wouldn't accept them. Before he hung up, he had literally gotten approval to scratch out everything he wanted out. Bernie knew his business and could be trusted with any deal I would bring before him. At the end of this conversation, he had arranged for a closing date at Value Line's offices just three days later.

When Bernie and I walked into their offices and sat down in an enormous boardroom to close the deal, everyone was elated about Bernie's corrections to the agreement and agreed to sign the acceptance papers. That $269,000 check from Value Line (received under the revised contract terms, thanks to Bernie) was the beginning of Aerosystems expansion.

After Bernie and I left Value Line's office, he took me over to the Fulton Fish Market, where we had a couple of deliciously fresh Dover sole fish dinners and celebrated with a bottle of the best wine the house had to offer.

As soon as I returned to New Jersey, I called Warren Beach, Jr., then president of Eclipse Systems, and told him that I was ready to fulfill the terms of my option by delivering a check in the amount of $150,000, together with Aerosystems stock, which was then trading at $5.50 per share.

I guess when I arrived at Eclipse the following day, Warren had had a hard time coming to the conclusion that he would no longer own the company. However, the cash was attractive and within an hour's time, Warren had signed my self-prepared acquisition agreement. That used to make Jay Benenson, our New Jersey lawyer, cringe. Fortunately, my ongoing working relationship with Bernie in his office gave me a knack for preparing exceptionally good legal contracts, and I always made sure they said what I wanted to hear. That way, at least, I would be satisfied and it would have to be the deal's opponent who would have to ask for modifications. If I didn't like it, I'd refuse to accept it. Although Bernie never mentioned it, I sensed he was reasonably satisfied that the contracts I had prepared were sufficient to protect my part of the deal.

After the acquisition of Eclipse, I left my offices in Franklin and spent a good part of the day in Fairfield, a town next to Wayne, where Eclipse was located. Warren Beach continued as president, and I spent my time privately speaking to many of the employees who really knew what was going on, mostly production workers. I could see the inefficiencies in the operation of the office because almost everyone did exactly as he pleased with little leadership.

I had to educate myself about the day-to-day operations. Costs lacked the proper controls. Items were not bought at the lowest prices with the best payment terms. For me, the purchasing criteria was the key to improving Eclipse's cash flow because, as it turned out, Eclipse was paying its bills in 90 to 120 days and vendors were getting impatient. It was evident that management had to pay closer attention to the daily business operations, including personnel.

The time came to find a new president of Eclipse or risk losing the business. Value Line would not take that lightly.

Shortly after 10 o'clock on a Monday morning I asked for the president's resignation. He seemed relieved to hear my request. I invited him into a side office I had set up for my sporadic day-to-day visits. I believe he felt that since he had a sizable stake in Aerosystems' public stock, resigning would at least protect his Aerosystems investment.

Warren had the rental income from Eclipse's building, and his father had left him a comfortable home on Martha's Vineyard.

Art Brukhardt, Vice President of Technology General,
receiving congratulations from Eclipse attorney.
Charles Fletcher far right.

He could retire there and take up his hobby of photography without further worry. We agreed that we would continue to pay him half of his salary for a period of six months after his departure.

For the next four weeks, I designated myself as President and Chief Operating Officer of Eclipse Systems and started having daily meetings with all key shop personnel and all office department heads. I also took control of purchasing and insisted on signing all purchase orders before a vendor was accepted. Within a month, purchases started to slow down while billing slightly improved.

At that particular time, my old boss at Reaction Motors, Arthur Brukardt, who had managed the Systems Engineering Group for the development of the X-15 rocket engine, was at home in Lake Hopatcong seeking a new job. Reaction Motors had been purchased by Thiokol Chemical Company that decided to close Reaction Motors. Thiokol decided to transfer everything, including a few remaining employees, back to Utah where their main solid rocket boosters were being made and tested for the National Aeronautics Space Administration (NASA). Working for Art as a Systems Project Engineer, I learned to respect his management talent and decided to give him a call. Art agreed to come in for an interview and a tour of the plant. It had been more than six years since I had left Reaction Motors to start Aerosystems on a full-time basis, so this meeting was something special for me.

Except for his being a few years older, Art and I seemed to hit it off. I offered him the job, starting with a modest salary subject to change based upon Eclipse's ability to improve cash flow, sales, and a return to growth. This was a great opportunity for Art, and his home was no more than thirty minutes from Eclipse's Fairfield plant.

Over the next six months Eclipse began to improve dramatically. During these few months, Art discovered that our purchasing agent was taking kickbacks from several suppliers. He was allowing vendors to inflate their prices for goods so he could realize the difference. Art told me one of the suppliers had called and thought that he was talking to our Purchasing Manager. The vendor then told Art where to meet him so that he could pay him a kickback in cash. This conversation opened up a Pandora's Box.

As soon as the conversation was over, Art called me at my Franklin office and asked me to rush down to Fairfield. Before I arrived, Art had pulled the last thirty or so purchases from Eclipse's files and had begun checking the prices with competitors. He also called the vendor whose name was on the invoice and used a fictitious company name to get another price quote on the items. After researching the first ten purchase orders, Art found that prices had been inflated between 20 and 30 percent, which indicated that the difference was undoubtedly going to the purchasing agent as a kickback.

After I arrived at Eclipse and reviewed Art's findings, we decided to spend the next two weeks evaluating every purchase made over the prior six months. Better than 90 percent of all purchases (especially large dollar items) carried a 20 to 25 percent inflation in price.

When Art and I decided that our agent was ripping off Eclipse, we called him into Art's office and immediately accused him of the kickback fraud. We had estimated that Eclipse had paid in excess of $90,000 more for its purchases than it should have and hence the primary reason for our cash flow problems.

The moment we charged our agent with fraud with his kickback scheme, his face became flushed like a tomato and ready to explode. He knew that he had been caught red-handed. He knew he was fired, but he didn't know if we were ready to charge him with theft.

Art and I came to the conclusion that making a criminal case out of this would be time-consuming and probably would not result in a recovery of our lost money without expending considerable time and effort prosecuting our agent. Instead, we told him that he would have to pay Eclipse $5,000 cash, forfeit a week's pay, and surrender his company car. Realizing that this was better than being charged with a criminal offense, he agreed to the deal and was terminated.

When word got around about the termination, the attitude of the remaining employees changed remarkably. They began taking their jobs seriously.

About a week later, I offered Art the position of President of Eclipse Systems and gave him full authority to hire and fire as he saw fit. Over the next six months, we called the major vendors who had participated in the kickback scheme and forced them to settle their payable accounts for as little as fifty cents on the dollar. Through that arrangement we recovered most of our losses without expensive litigation.

Before the first full year was over, Art had reduced payables from well over $275,000 to as low as $75,000, and sales with the military began increasing. Eclipse Systems was now a highly profitable company and helping Aerosystems, the parent company, reduce its $300,000 small business loan debt.

20

A Win-Win
with
Whippany Electronics

$\mathcal{M}$etaltec Corporation, which I was managing behind the scenes back in Franklin, was growing nicely by manufacturing writing instrument components and cosmetic metal bottle caps.

While at Metaltec, I was still working with John Padalino, President of Whippany electronics who continued to manufacture my "Power Plus" speed control. Having just completed the acquisition of Eclipse Systems, Inc., also located in Fairfield, New Jersey, I began talking daily to John about the opportunities of Whippany also becoming a public company. This immediately interested him, so we structured a deal whereby John would give me 15 percent of his Whippany stock provided I could talk our New York attorney, Bernie Coven, into doing a Regulation A Public Offering for $300,000 just as he did for Technology General.

Again, over the next several months working into the early hours of the morning, we soon compiled all the necessary corporate, legal, and financial documents required for the Securities and Exchange Commission (SEC). Satisfied all the documents were in order, Bernie, representing Whippany Electronics including my 15 percent interest, agreed to sign an Underwriting Agreement with Nagler and Wiesman to raise $300,000 of public funds before expenses.

For me this effort to underwrite Whippany Electronics seemed like a real opportunity to acquire 15 percent of a new public company stock.

I recalled my high school classroom motto, "Seize the Opportunity," a positive thought that always stays in the back of my mind.

Padalino was an extremely savvy engineer who had somehow developed the popular music combo organs while working for a company called Magnus. After leaving Magnus he developed a new prototype organ that became a huge success, which resulted in the expansion of Whippany Electronics.

Before the underwriting issue of SEC was approved, underwriters Nagler and Weisman had oversold the Whippany Electronics issue. Soon Whippany Electronics became a public company with $280,000 cash in the bank. Having all this newfound equity capital, Whippany rapidly expanded its electronic organ sales (the "Melo-Sonic") to well over $2 million in sales.

As the pressure of running a public company began to rise, John came to me and said, "I think it would be best for me if Whippany was acquired by Aerosystems. If you would agree to exchange my Whippany stock for Aero stock, I will agree to merge our companies." Completely surprised by this comment and thinking over the idea, I saw an opportunity to again double the size of our Aerosystems Technology. Besides, John said he would rather concentrate on Research and Development than worry about running the new public company. Again, discussing this acquisition with Bernie, legal work was initiated to complete the merger. Soon Whippany Electronics was a wholly owned subsidiary of the parent Aerosystems Technology causing our stock to rise well over six dollars a share.

We soon set up a distributorship and warehouse in Montreal. As sales increased with our new line of organ models, I arranged for a loan of $150,000 with the Imperial Bank of Canada to help finance the Canadian inventory. Since the Canadian bank had a New York branch, their vice president of corporate loans decided to visit our plant in Franklin. When he arrived at my office, I recalled him introducing himself as "William" but forgot his last name.

Padalino and I decided to take William to lunch at the new Playboy Club at McAfee, up the road from Franklin six miles from our plant. Their executive dining room was quite the setting to impress William in an atmosphere where half a dozen Playboy Bunnies kept drifting by serving all your dining needs. The purpose of this meeting, of course, was to tell William about our Whippany Melo-Sonic organ sales expansion in Canada, which was the reason for the $150,000 bank loan.

Everything had been going along breezily, impressing William at every opportunity with our rapid expansion and plans for added growth in the huge Canadian marketplace, when the one and only male waiter presented me with the check. In my usual business manner, I flipped open my wallet and presented the waiter with my American Express Card. As we sat there waiting for him to return with my credit card, it seemed like a month of Sundays. At last he returned and leaned over to whisper in my ear, "Sorry, sir, your credit card is no good." As my complexion swiftly passed through the vivid colors of the rainbow, I didn't know what to say and even worse, I knew William knew what was happening, and to make matters even more painful I had so little cash on me that I was approaching a state of shock.

William, snickering in a forgiving way, realized the embarrassing position I was in and generously agreed to pay the bill. While William was paying, I tried my best to let him know that there must have been a mistake with my American Express account, and that I expected to get to the bottom of this unusual situation just as soon as I returned to my office. Fortunately for John and me, on the way back to the office, William said, "You know, I can understand how you feel. I've had the same thing happen to me." He assured me, "not to worry about a thing. Your loan with our bank is as good as gold. We will forward our check for $150,000 to Whippany early next week."

The loan arrived on time and allowed us to increase our Canadian sales over the next fourteen months, enabling us to pay

John Padalino (left), President of Whippany Electronics, Inc. and Charles J. Fletcher (right), President of Technology General Corp. at a trade show in New York.

off the Canadian loan in full long before its due date. When we made our last payment, William said, "Charlie I knew you two guys would make good because you demonstrated to me your product was really ready for a hot, new market."

For the next year sales remained steady until the Japanese came out with higher priced models that started to cut into our market. The Japanese eventually started undercutting our prices to the point where John Padalino began to see the handwriting on the wall.

Unfortunately, John reacted negatively to our parent company's efforts to analyze the problems and to minimize the ever-increasing losses from foreign competition. John then aligned himself with a competitor who encouraged him to join his company called Artisan Electronics. Within six months, John had taken our technology over to Artisan and began producing exact copies of our organs.

Our directors insisted on suing John for taking our trade secrets. This litigation cost both of us considerable money, and because of a lack of bona fide U.S. patents, the judge called it a draw and allowed John to continue providing certain visual styling changes to the beleaguered musical machine. Over the next six months, neither company could make any real headway, trying to compete with the Japanese on a profitable basis.

Four months later, a friend called me and told me that John had passed away after a sudden heart attack. Although John and I had our differences, I had always respected him for his hands-on approach to developing new products without the usual time-consuming design stages. John always knew what he wanted to produce and went ahead and built it from a pile of junk until it performed exactly as if it were worth thousands more because of sophisticated engineering designs.

After John's death, his widow, Evelyn, started putting things back together but held negative feelings toward me for several years. As the beneficiary of John's stock in our firm, Aerosystems Technology (the parent), she attended our annual stockholder meetings and was the only person to vote against me and management in general. After a few years, she started her own small printing business and for reasons unknown, slowly became one of my dearest friends. Looking back, I guess she began to realize the steps I had recommended to fight off the Japanese competitors had not been so bad after all. To this day, we are still best of friends, and I continue to support her business interests. Since she currently owns the small printing business, our company offers her our printing requirements every chance we get.

21

The Big Fire
of 1977

*I*t was May 7, 1977. Everything was going reasonably well. Our public offering was successful in late 1968, the acquisition of Eclipse Systems enhanced our growth through sales increase with an expanded industrial product market, and the acquisition of Whippany Electronics Inc. broadened our capabilities with a growth rate jumping in excess of 300 percent.

It was around 2:30 in the afternoon when one our employees on the finishing floor of Metaltec yelled "FIRE!" Within minutes all our employees began evacuating the plant, the site where environmental problems had begun to emerge. It wasn't more than fifteen minutes when it became apparent that the second floor also had to be abandoned because of the intense heat. Minutes later the Franklin and Hamburg Fire Departments responded. It was obvious that the entire cosmetic finishing department was going to be destroyed. By 5 p.m. that day, the firemen got the blaze well under control, but there was no doubt in our minds that Metaltec's finishing department would be inoperable for several months.

When the fire recovery activity was well underway, we learned from a local attorney friend, Donald Kovach, that just two miles away, a company known as Cellate, Inc., owned by a firm in England, had abandoned a sizable plant and forty-four acres that had been developed on a rock base of a former limestone quarry. Because of the serious damage to our company, I decided to investigate the Cellate property as a new potential home for Metaltec. Following the Metaltec fire we became concerned about what appeared to be contaminated land caused by tenant companies prior to our purchase in 1964. As it turned out, the property was free of contamination.

While the Cellate property itself was somewhat messy and the building required a great deal of refurbishing to meet our Metaltec needs, I decided to call the Cellate main office in Newark to see what price they would be asking since the property had been abandoned. I surmised that the Cellate management might be glad to sell it at a reduced price. After calling it was apparent they really wanted a buyer at any price. Since we were about to get an insurance reimbursement for the Metaltec fire, it was a propitious time to use this money for a property expansion, if at all feasible.

Following a number of exploratory discussions, I began to suspect that a non-cash deal would be of interest. This would be ideal for Metaltec because it was necessary to get the plant up and running as quickly as possible. After several conversations, Cellate's lawyer said, "Would you be willing to give us a part payment in Aerosystems public stock with the balance in cash?" Subject to the price for the plant and forty-four beautiful acres, I replied, "possibly."

As negotiations progressed, Cellate's lawyers said that to speed the deal, their board of directors would take a price of $200,000 comprising $100,000 in stock and $100,000 in cash. This wasn't too bad if I could get a decent market value for our over-the-counter stock in Aerosystems Technology, the parent company at that time. Checking our OTC market, Aerosystems was trading around $4 per share. That meant if Cellate would agree to the market price of $100,000, we would pay almost 50 percent of the Cellate acquisition for 25,000 shares of Aerosystems with the balance ($100,000) to be paid off over four years on a mortgage. After we talked to our Midlantic bankers in Newark about the deal, they agreed that if the property was environmentally sound, they would back the deal and make additional funds available for property and building restoration.

Former Cellate property redeveloped by Technology General (1997) and our home after the fire.

Armed with the bank's support, I thought I would try once more to encourage a price drop, so I called the Cellate attorney and said, "We will give you $100,000 in stock at $4 per share (25,000 shares) and $100,000 on a mortgage note payable over six years. Interest cannot exceed 7 percent and this offer is final. Unless we hear from you by tomorrow noon this offer is cancelled."

Within two hours the Cellate attorney called back and said, "You drive a hard bargain, but you've got a deal. Set up an immediate closing."

Within a week, the Aerosystems stock of 25,000 shares were issued to Cellate, and the Midlantic Bank made ample funds available after we received an appraisal of $675,000 on property purchased with an expenditure of only $100,000, payable over six long years, representing a substantial security spread to cover additional borrowed funds.

Over the next two months, we stripped the property of all debris, refurbished the buildings, and began moving Metaltec operations into the new facility. Over the following eighteen months we rebuilt the burned out Metaltec plant and rented the space. At the same time we constructed new executive offices at an existing Cellate plant and doubled the plant size for Eclipse Systems. And with the help of fifteen Metaltec employees and a crackerjack maintenance chief with industrial construction experience, Metaltec added a 35,000 foot new facility that was up and operational within five months. These fifteen guys would work their Metaltec shift from 7 a.m. until 3:30 p.m., then start plant construction from 4:30 to 9:00 at night using bank-borrowed funds to pay for their loyal effort. To keep this construction going each afternoon, we would buy two cases of beer "on the house." What a fabulous job the guys did to get the Metaltec operation back up and running. Within a period of two years from the date of acquisition, the former Cellate abandoned facility became a model industrial park, which subsequently led to Aerosystems Technology winning a prestigious Industrial Development Award from President Ronald Reagan.

Meanwhile, the former Metaltec plant site was rebuilt with insurance funds, and a few good tenants emerged to sustain our much-needed income. However, beyond all this the New Jersey Department of Environmental Protection Agency began to uncover large areas of contamination that the former tenants buried beneath a parking area. Unfortunately, this unexpected environmental nightmare was about to raise its ugly head.

22

Expanding Our
Industrial Development

*A*gain, those same words, "Seize the Opportunity," became the focus of my imagination. About 1979, our industrial enterprises were running smoothly. All of our subsidiaries were holding their own. However, nothing positive or exciting was really happening related to our burning desire to grow by way of corporate acquisitions.

One afternoon as I was standing in the lobby of the Bank of Sussex County, our local financial institution, I overheard a young man, obviously an attorney, ask the teller, "Do you know or perhaps your bank president would know any local real estate developers who may be interested in buying a nearby farm with 106 acres?"

The teller, noticing me and realizing I had overheard the conversation, instantly directed the lawyer to me, saying, "Mr. Fletcher is standing right over there. He has an ever-expanding industrial company. Perhaps he may show some interest."

Walking toward me, he introduced himself as Mr. Feltman. He began to tell me a story of 106 acres nearby that was owned by his 89-year-old grandmother. He said his grandmother just took back this land resulting from a mortgage foreclosure. Because of her advanced age, she was eager to find a new buyer because she needed the money. Evidently, it was the only remaining asset she possessed. Being fully aware that Sussex County, the area where I lived and worked, was beginning to show signs of growth, I asked Mr. Feltman how much his grandmother was asking for the property. Well, he said she last sold it at $2,700 per acre; he realized, however, that the problem of getting a new buyer would present a problem she wasn't prepared to deal with. He then asked me if I were interested in making an offer. Knowing that no matter what I asked, she would likely raise the price anyhow, I said the best I could do on short notice was $700 an acre. Smiling, he came right back saying, "I don't think she could accept that kind of reduction in price. However, I will take it up with her and call you." Exchanging business cards, we both departed and went about our business.

About four days later, I got a call from Mr. Feltman who said his grandmother would not accept $700 an acre, but she would accept $1,050 per acre and "give you a mortgage at 8 percent." That answer almost knocked me off my feet because two days earlier I had learned that this property was the town's choice for a modern industrial park with both sewer and water, a commodity unheard of in Sussex County. Being coy, I responded that I would talk to my bank and get back to him shortly.

Before I hung up, I knew this property was clean farmland with access bordering on two major roadways providing excellent industrial access to that valuable tract of land. I could not wait for the following day, and I didn't even have to consult my banker. That was only an excuse so as not to appear too eager. Determined to make some change, I called him up and said, "If your grandmother will cut the interest to 7 percent instead of 8, I would be able to offer $1,150 an acre instead of $1,050, as long as she would take no cash in advance and give me a seven-year mortgage."

After a brief delay, Mr. Feltman called back saying I "drive a hard bargain." However, his grandmother would agree providing he prepared all the mortgage documents.

One week later, Technology General was the owner of 106 acres of industrial zoned land with great potential for a minimum of fifteen industrial plant sites.

As luck would have it, the Feltman farmland remained an untouched investment for about seven years when the town fathers, in cooperation with an adjacent property owner, agreed to provide three new deep wells for a tap water supply for his proposed housing development. This agreement would allow the Borough of Franklin to use this abundant new water supply for the town's future development needs. Fortunately, to provide this water to the town it became necessary to bring the main water supply line directly through the center of the Feltman property. In the interim, Technology General presented a plan to the town for a new high-tech Industrial Park called the Franklin Corporate Campus. The new upscale corporate park would provide 15 industrial plant sites on 106 acres. With this water line in place at a cost to the town of $940,000, our new Corporate Campus value was reappraised from $160,000 to $2.6 million. This project is presently seeking state permits for commercial development projected at $30 million.

23

Taking a Piece
of "The Rock"

*I*t wasn't six months after the Feltman deal I got a call from a Prudential Insurance Company representative who was holding title to a 100,000-square-foot plant abandoned by American Urethane. American Urethane was reportedly having extreme problems with their labor union.

By the time I got this call from Prudential, the building had already been abandoned seven or eight months and was showing wear. Coincidentally, this plant was adjacent to the recently-acquired 106-acre Feltman property. It was an ideal acquisition to our proposed industrial park — the Franklin Corporate Campus.

When Prudential's representative called, he told me that he recently learned that I was the only industrialist in Sussex County with the ability to take over a building this size. When I asked the representative what price he was asking, he said somewhere around one million six hundred thousand. Laughing out loud, I returned his answer by saying, "Where the devil do you expect a small hometown guy like me to get that kind of money?" So he said, "Well, make me an offer." Thinking about it a moment, I blurted out, "I'd consider $350,000." A quick answer came back, "What, are you crazy? Thanks but no thanks." Then the phone went dead. Obviously, he hung up in disgust at my offer.

About five months had gone by and when I drove by the Prudential building, I noticed the real estate sign was still in place. Happily for me, there had been no serious offers.

One day the office phone rang and my secretary, Lyn Hopler, said a Prudential representative is calling again. The same guy said, "Let's be realistic. Make me an offer I can accept, and I will help you finance the whole project, including refurbishing funds."

Realizing that he was having difficult liquidation problems, I said, "I'll make an offer of $450,000, provided you arrange a low-interest New Jersey Economic Development Finance Bond with interest no more than 7 percent. Again, he told me it wasn't good enough and once more hung up.

A week later, for the third time, the Prudential representative called and when Lyn put the call through, I said without thinking, "You discourteous bastard, you hung up on me for the last time." And I slammed the phone down in his ear.

It wasn't five minutes later he called back to say he was sorry for the way he hung up as he was under severe pressure to get a sale completed. Sensing a good deal was beginning to take form, I accepted his apology and asked what he wanted. He answered that his board of directors would agree if I would accept $575,000 and they would guarantee a loan for $800,000 so I could renovate the building. To keep him on that aggressive line, I said I'd talk to my banker at Midlantic and then call him back. A quick call confirmed the bank's approval of the deal, so the acquisition process was again in motion.

Before closing the deal firmly with Prudential, I thought I would press him one more time for an important mortgage modification. Calling the Prudential rep I said, "If you agree to conduct a complete environmental study on the surrounding plant land and pay for a total of seven monitoring wells, you have a deal subject to successful environmental results." He said, "We can't hold up this closing, but we will agree that if for any reason the environmental tests are unfavorable, we will indemnify Technology General." Also, he would agree to accept our first payment upon

Jersey City Mayor Gerald McCann (right), Charles J. Fletcher, President and Chief Executive Officer, Aerosystems Technology Corp. (center), and Kendall Wayne Lampkin (left), Special Assistant to the Regional Administrator, U.S. Department of Housing and Urban Development. Aerosystems Technology Corp. receives a Presidential Recognition Award for volunteer activities benefiting neighborhood communities in New Jersey.

Charles J. Fletcher in his office.

Prudential Building.

completion of the test results. With that, I agreed to the deal provided the latter conditions were placed in the mortgage papers.

The closing day approached. We met in the Prudential real estate offices in Newark. We signed the papers and took control over a Midlantic bank check for the full $800,000. Because we did not have to pay Prudential until the results of the environmental study were complete, I endorsed the Midlantic check for $800,000, with payments now at 8 percent for interest, then handing the check back to Midlantic, I redeposited the funds into our corporate account that would pay immediate interest at 14.5 percent.

What a hell of a deal. After the process started to sink in, Prudential said, "Wait a minute! You're making a lot of interest on our money!"

I fired back, "No, you get your money as stated in the agreement AFTER acceptance of the samples from the seven monitoring wells, provided they pass all the DEP tests."

Prudential began to see what a stupid clause they agreed to. As it turned out, it took approximately seventeen months for the wells to be approved. This delay allowed us to retain the $575,000 purchase price deposit for a period of 17 months, which at 6.5 percent interest spread between the borrowed rate (8.5) and the deposit rate (14.5) for a period of 17 months generated a net gain of $53,625. The balance of $225,000 was spent on immediate plant renovations.

The primary significance of this Prudential building acquisition was that its southern boundary lay directly adjacent to the entry of the former Feltman 106 acres. This geographical coincidence made it possible to develop a grand entrance into the 106-acre site for the Franklin Corporate Campus. My industrial campus master plan envisioned a total of fifteen industrial plant sites, a project the town and county wholly endorsed.

With the blessing of the town fathers at the Franklin Planning/Zoning Board's level, this property has now been legally memorialized for development. With the recently-acquired 106,000 square-foot structure called the Munsonhurst building adjacent to its property entrance, it is being projected as a huge future ratable and a major industrial redevelopment, which the town lost with the closing down of its New Jersey zinc mines in the early 1950s.

Technology General Corporation, my new parent company, was now becoming a major employment base, a modern successor to the legendary Franklin Zinc Mines where my father, grandfather, uncles, and other relatives worked all of their lives.

The following year, the Sussex County Board of Chosen Freeholders held an industrial dinner event. It was at this event at the former Playboy Club Hotel in McAfee, New Jersey, where Technology General was named the Industrial Achiever of the Year. Shortly thereafter, I was given the annual President Reagan Industrial Development Award for the ability to reclaim abandoned industrial properties to activate community ratable gains and countywide employment.

As of June 1, 2000, we began construction of a new 10,500 square foot addition to accommodate $2.5 million in new high-tech machinery.

24

The Endless Environmental Nightmare

*D*uring the late 1970s, my parent company, Aerosystems Technology Corporation, was still operating out of the same plant in Franklin where our subsidiary, Metaltec Corporation, still manufactured metal writing instrument components and a variety of metal cosmetic caps. Some of our best customers were Sheaffer Pen, Papermate, Revlon, and Fabergé.

About 300 yards from the plant was a lagoon, which Metaltec used to transfer its detergent wash water used to clean the metal components.

One summer day in 1978, two New Jersey State Department of Environmental Protection (DEP) officials showed up at the door and said they had evidence from a few local residents that Metaltec was dumping toxic waste into the lagoon. That day was the beginning of continuous harassment from both state and federal government officials that is still going on as I write this some twenty-two years later.

Since the government environmental officials showed up at my office that year, Aerosystems Technology and, currently, Technology General Corporation, have experienced a continuous decline in business, one that threatens our future as a viable company.

At the time we acquired the property, there were no state or federal "Superfund" cleanup laws or any significant laws that called for disposal of various forms of industrial waste. In 1978, Metaltec was located on an isolated parcel of property away from our current corporate offices and industrial park. For years, Metaltec discharged water from the plant to rinse metal components with a special high-strength industrial soap, which was permitted by local and state authorities to flow into a shallow man-made lagoon having a clay bottom to help inhibit filtration into the ground. Here the water would evaporate, and the lagoon would act as an exposed septic system, which was periodically treated chemically to remove algae growth and other unpleasant odors.

The visit by the State Department of Environmental Protection was the beginning of an unending twenty-two-year horror story. The initial DEP discussion seemed insignificant at the time. The only concern the DEP inspector expressed was that we make sure the lagoon would not overflow. He also asked to test the water in sample jars he provided.

About a month later, the DEP inspector returned and said the samples taken from our lagoon were okay, but nearby neighbors were complaining because they believed pollution was being discharged into the environment.

Unbeknownst to the company, there was a local group of environmentalists made up primarily of a few neighbors. One of these individuals happened to be a chemist. Several times one of our local employees caught him taking pictures in the vicinity of the lagoon. We went so far as to suspect him of deliberately spiking the lagoon with a toxic chemical of the trichloroethylene family because he knew the product was used in our plant for cleaning the metal pens and cosmetic components.

In due time we learned this environmental infiltrator had written a letter to the New Jersey Environmental Commissioner, requesting that a team of inspectors visit the surrounding seven acres for any potential signs of contamination. Although I was satisfied the company was operating the lagoon by discharging a biodegradable detergent, I had no idea what the surrounding acreage would contain, if anything.

Shortly after the team of inspectors arrived, it was learned that the prior tenant of the building, a firm known as Accurate Forming Corporation, had leased the building before our company Metaltec was founded. It was also learned from many of our employees, by written affidavits, that Accurate Forming stored its toxic waste in the building because Andrew Serin, at that time, was one of the partners of Accurate Forming while the company operated nearby in Ogdensburg. Not long after Serin leased the building to Accurate, the principals decided to part company with Serin. In retaliation, Serin forced Accurate Forming to remove its stored chemical waste in his building to allow him to begin his own business, Marmike Manufacturing, in direct competition with Accurate Forming. For whatever reason, Accurate management talked Serin into allowing them to excavate a quarter-acre site about 150 yards from the plant on the opposite side of the road, then hired a contractor friend of Serin to excavate a substantial hole and bury the stored waste from the building they leased, all unbeknownst to Aerosystems at the time of its purchase of the property in late 1965.

A year later, Marmike went into bankruptcy and was renamed Serin Enterprises. As you will recall, I acquired Serin Enterprise assets in 1964, including seven acres of the Serin property surrounding the plant and incorporated Serin into Metaltec Corporation.

Not until 1978, when the DEP inspectors arrived to conduct a thorough search of the property, did I or anyone else in our company know of this massive dumping by Accurate Forming years earlier.

This investigation developed into an intensive check of the nearby groundwater and resulted in numerous core samplings of the dumped soil. This became so serious that Franklin Borough's new town well was completely shut down, and several nearby neighbors' private wells were tested and found contaminated.

About a month later, Franklin Borough sued Aerosystems. Aerosystems countersued the Borough because their ten-year dump site was located less than a quarter-of-a-mile from the plant site. Three neighbors also filed suit for polluted wells, kicking off three years of litigation that began to devastate the company with excessive legal costs.

As a show of good faith, I elected to start cleanup excavation and pay for the polluted site across the road from the plant. Also our company agreed to discontinue the use of the lagoon, excavate the dirt, refill with fresh soil, and pay for the disposal. The total cost to the company, including legal costs by 1982, exceeded $835,000. These funds came from a little nest egg that was helping the company to expand before the event began.

Late in 1982 or early 1983, Aerosystems settled all its litigation, collected a few hundred thousand dollars from an insurance company, paid for the town well, paid off three neighbors for releases, and thought the problem would go away forever.

Not so. Before the end of 1984, the State of New Jersey placed our property on the Superfund List of Hazardous Waste Cleanups, which was tantamount to a doctor examining you for cancer and declaring you terminally ill.

Superfund was created by Congress in 1981 to clean up America's hazardous waste sites. That set off a federal expenditure program that has now redone, unnecessarily, everything Aerosystems accomplished for the DEP under the DEP's full and continuous supervision. The cost to taxpayers as I write this is now in excess of $12.7 million and, believe it or not, a new program is about to start that will aerate the groundwater for at least another five years at a cost projected well in excess of another $3.5 million.

Only recently the results of this water purification program revealed that sixty-five tons of earth had been shipped to a waste management division in Michigan at a cost exceeding several hundred thousand dollars.

Fortuitously, one day in early February 2000, a package arrived in the mail addressed to Technology General, a package we later learned was intended to go to the EPA. What a mistake the management firm in Michigan made because it was discovered in the test report that all sixty-five tons were determined to

be in their own words, NONHAZARDOUS, NONTOXIC AND
NONREGULATED MATERIAL. What a financial blow this is to
the taxpayer, and we are sure there will be more shipments to follow. These papers will be used as evidence in our upcoming case
and, until then, they will remain in high security as evidence of
extravagantly wasteful expenditures for no apparent reason.

Ironically, my cousin, Gordon Bishop, was the catalyst for
the nation's first "State Spill Fund" in 1976 and the subsequent
Federal "Superfund" law in 1981. It was his pioneering investigation as an environmental reporter and columnist for *The Star-
Ledger*, New Jersey's largest newspaper, that brought about these
industrial reforms. An award-winning investigation Gordon
launched in November 1975 led to the closing of the nation's
first chemical garbage dump in Edison, New Jersey. The dump,
called Kin-Buc, was then closed by the DEP in February 1976,
leading to New Jersey's "State Spill Fund," the forerunner of the
federal Superfund. New Jersey State Senator Raymond Lesniak,
and New Jersey Congressman Jim Florio, both Democrats,
developed the State Spill Fund and Federal Superfund legislation, respectively.

Gordon said his response to the Kin-Buc "ticking time
bomb" was to clean up the site with appropriate and affordable
technology. Government had other ideas, however, which turned
out to be a national environmental and financial disaster for both
taxpayers and industry.

In Gordon's New Jersey syndicated column, ON THE
ISSUES, published in December 1999, he apologized to New Jersey's business community for what happened following the Kin-
Buc cleanup legislation. "What started out as a sound, reasonable
method of cleaning up hazardous waste was turned into a prohib-
itively expensive cleanup caused by environmental lawyers and
bureaucrats who created an uncontrollable regulatory system that
spent 90 percent of Superfund monies on paperwork and only 10
percent in actual remediation of toxic sites."

"The Superfund program involves more than $50 billion
worth of cleanups in America. That figure could even escalate to

more than $100 billion as more and more sites are discovered throughout the nation," he wrote.

That's not what Gordon's investigation of a chemical garbage dump had intended. After my cousin's humble "public apology" for something over which he had no control — namely, government bureaucrats — one can now understand why it is easy to distrust the empire-building Superfund bureaucracy. For example, the whole surrounding twenty-two acres Aerosystems purchased was appraised by the bureaucrats at only $2,500 an acre or a paltry $55,000.

Superfund devalues business assets and inflates the costs of cleanups. Superfund became a classic government bureaucratic disaster, representing the worst of both worlds — the public and private sectors.

Even worse, after hundreds of thousands of dollars of well and groundwater tests, the federal Environmental Protection Agency (EPA) declared at its public hearing:

"Although the groundwater has been found to contain small traces of toxic material, it is believed that it will not cause a detrimental long-term effect to game, fish, plant vegetation or surrounding wetlands. However, it is our firm opinion it is in the interest of the public to carry out the intent of the entire proposed program."

The government thus has a right to continue the expansion of this vast environmental network despite any apparent need. Other examples of enormous government waste of funds were revealed from our own in-depth research and investigation. Shortly after one of the EPA excavation phases began, a contractor showed up and placed a high cyclone fence around a quarter-of-an-acre excavation work site. Naturally being inquisitive, I took it upon myself to ask an employee of the engineering company how much his company paid for the erection of the fence. He replied he didn't think it was any of my business, but nevertheless did say it cost $57,000, and that it was erected by his Love Canal contractor-friend whose home base I learned was in Niagara Falls, New York.

Having placed similar fencing around Aerosystems new corporate site about a mile away, I decided to ask five well-known local fence contractors to bid the job already done by Severson's friend. Although they realized I could not give them the job already erected, I promised to pay them $75 each just to quote this fence job. All five came back with quotes within a week, revealing the low bidder price at $7,500 and the high bidder at $12,300. The high bidder said he bid high because he was busy and didn't really need the job.

Now it doesn't take any brains to realize at the lower bid price the government spent at least $49,500 more than they should have. Although I reported this private investigation to the EPA, they told me *they had no control over the contractor because he took the job at a fixed price.*

Remember that $835,000 cleanup Aerosystems accomplished back in 1982 and 1983, all under State of New Jersey DEP supervision? Some 30 or 40 tandem truckloads of excavated waste were shipped to Maryland by a certified hauler under controlled DEP trucking manifests that recorded every detail. According to EPA's own plan, Severson Engineering excavated tons of *clean* fill I replaced for the DEP in 1982-1983 and shipped my clean fill all the way to Michigan.

I had warned the contractor that I had replaced this excavation area with clean fill. I asked him why do this before testing the soil? His brief answer was, "they pay me handsomely for doing it, and I don't give a damn if the dirt I had replaced was clean."

It wasn't six months after Severson Engineering completed its excavation of the area that I had already cleaned up for the DEP when a report showed up in our mail. It was addressed to Metaltec Corporation, c/o Severson Engineering. Without thinking much about it, Lyn Hopler, my observant secretary, opened the large envelope only to find the test results of the Severson Engineering excavation. She handed it to me for review. This report and a second report received earlier recorded in excess of 2,300 tests from the Severson excavation for just about every known toxic chemical imaginable. We reviewed the results on every page. Along each side was recorded an "ND," which we learned from a code at the bottom of the page stood for "nondeterminable" for all tests but three items, each costing the government about $220. Estimated costs for soil testing was $506,000. Soil excavation was estimated to cost in excess of $600,000, and transporting the excavated soil to Michigan $750,000 for a total cost of $1,856,000.

Reading about the excessively wasteful practices of the federal Superfund process is tedious, beyond the patience of many taxpaying citizens, but I had to explain just a little of this maddening process, hoping our congressional leaders see the waste the Superfund causes in depleting our limited taxpayers dollars.

It has been widely documented that between 1985 and 1998, the Superfund follies literally destroyed thousands of small businesses and devastated an equal number of individuals who worked all their lives building businesses that were the backbone of America. Superfund actions forced many businesses to move to other countries that didn't have such unjust laws.

As I write, this government-caused mess still exists, spanning more than two decades. Because this costly problem has created such a potential liability for our companies, I have discouraged further efforts to expand our businesses.

By early 1990, Technology General Corporation faced litigation from both the DEP and the EPA, requesting payments exceeding $4.6 million for its cleanup expenditures, now ballooned to amounts in excess of $12.5 million.

Although we have spent about $200,000 in legal fees over this period, we have been fortunate to have our dear friend, attorney Jay Benenson, agree to fight this case. From the beginning Jay was an unusually capable attorney who became the company's loyal general counsel. When we acquired this contaminated property back in the early 1960s there were no environmental laws in place.

In early August 2000 Jay advised me that the Federal District Court in Newark was reviewing the case for trial. The State Attorney General had refused to join in a "Global Settlement" with the federal EPA to resolve our full Superfund issue once and for all.

Fortunately for the company and me, we had a fair and rational federal judge who seemed to loathe the excessive pressure government bureaucrats applied to literally destroy a healthy company. In an effort to counter this bureaucratic effort, he would scold them severely and insist they retire to one of his conference rooms to hammer out an equitable settlement that would allow the defendant to survive. Usually, his final words were "Don't come out until you have a just solution because I refuse to try this case in this Federal Court."

As of this writing, the federal and state governments appear to be backing off sufficiently to allow us settlement terms based on our projected cash flow. We are thus looking forward to liquidating our former Superfund site including the plant at a price that will accommodate substantially 85 percent of the contemplated one million dollar settlement. This is considered an equitable settlement when we realize the total cleanup liability is now in excess of $19 million. Of course once the bureaucrats have free rein on your checkbook after declaring a Superfund, guilty or not the costs can be astronomical.

Thanks to the Federal judge's persistence, this case is now approaching a final settlement. It is my belief that only God could have assigned us such a fair-minded judge who saw merit in protecting our long-term welfare in the interest of saving many jobs and potential growth in the town of Franklin that more often than not suffers from economic depression.

25

Return of the Glidemobile as the Hovercraft

*W*hat a surprise to see my Glidemobile once again making the national news in 1960, this time on the cover of *Design News*. Other articles were subsequently published in *Aviation Week* and *Aero Digest*, two leading aeronautical magazines.

But it was no longer the Glidemobile. What I was looking at in these magazines was a hybrid version identified as the "Hovercraft."

Several years had gone by since the Glidemobile captured the public's attention. During that time the British had made major inroads toward the development of a large capacity military and commercial passenger-carrying waterborne vehicle.

The first version of the British prototype in a 1961 edition of *Aviation Week* came as a real shocker for those who worked with me to launch the Glidemobile. My friends and I were astounded at the similarities of the British version to the prototype we successfully flew for *Design News* prior to 1961. Vic Adams, my Reaction Motors associate, could not believe it — 95 percent of the Glidemobile's key design features were prominently visible on the British Hovercraft. The fins were nearly the same, the louver controls for directional control were copied exactly, and, more significantly, the inflatable rubber skirt, which was the basis for our disclosure to the U.S. Army, was essentially similar to the Glidemobile design.

It was a blatant rip-off of design and operational functions. Somewhere, somehow, a security breach had occurred at Fort Eustis, Virginia, where proprietary development and disclosure information about the "Glidemobile" concept was passed into the hands of the British after the military placed a security hold on our proposal.

Not realizing at the time the events that had taken place with our so-called confidential proposal, both Aerosystems, then its successor, Technology General, began to pursue a comprehensive plan for rapid growth.

As we pursued our industrial objectives for more than twenty-four years, an unusual telephone call came in to Beverly Jansen, my secretary, in early 1982. "There's a lawyer on the phone who says he's from the Justice Department and understands there may be a Charles J. Fletcher who works here."

Surprised and confused, I was extremely reluctant to take the call. Nevertheless, I asked Beverly to pass the call through, as my curiosity demanded to know what this was all about, regardless of the outcome.

The conversation began with my typically courteous, "Hello, may I help you?" The voice on the phone said something like this: "My name is Mr. Donald Townsend. I am an attorney with the Justice Department in Washington, D.C., assigned to a litigation case. It involves the British Hovercraft Company, which is suing the U.S. Government for royalties for a period of 1961 to 1982 regarding the Hovercraft development claimed to be invented by the British."

Following a brief pause, I asked Mr. Townsend, "How in the world did you find Aerosystems, and more specifically me?"

"Well," he said, "I went to the Library of Congress, being basically ignorant of the Hovercraft development. There I found this fantastic story about a Mr. Fletcher and the cover story of his development of the Glidemobile." Further he said, "Armed with this information, I called the operator in Newton, New Jersey, and asked her if she had ever heard of a company called Fletch-Aire. She had not, saying 'There is no company in Newton anymore by the name of Fletch-Aire.' She had, however, 'heard of a company over in nearby Franklin called Aerosystems,' which she believed 'is run by a fellow named Fletcher.' " Townsend then asked if the operator could give him the telephone number of Aerosystems.

Townsend and I thus became well acquainted. After considerable conversation, it was decided the Justice Department would send a team of high-powered specialists from the Office of Naval Research, the Navy Department, the Bureau of Ships, and the Smithsonian Institute to our company.

The following Monday, five people from these organizations entered my office at our new industrial complex. They were most curious. They wanted to know what technical evidence I still had in our files proving that the dates on the drawings were true and that the Glidemobile really flew over land and water, as I had related to Townsend. The proof was on the 16mm color film.

As the discussion began, I assured them that not only did I have a few of the original disclosure papers sent to the U.S. Army in Fort Eustis, Virginia, as a proposal for a contract, but I also had a file of technical data developed by Victor Adams, including the 16mm color film taken by Hardy Kircher.

Elated over the vast amount of Hovercraft development material and a film of the successful flight, they insisted on taking all of this data back to Washington to photograph and record for their upcoming litigation. Before they left my office that day, I made them agree to give me a signed, itemized receipt for all the documents and to assure me that the material would be returned within forty-five days, which they agreed to do. After all, it was now approximately twenty-five years since this material was sent to Fort Eustis when I was screwed by those who froze my patent into secrecy and when they failed to award the prototype development, which I had to fund myself with some friends.

A little over a month had passed when a second call came in from a Mr. Robert Alther, another attorney on the case who offered me a proposition. Alther said the material we gave the Justice Department was superior to anything else given them in their investigation to date, and that to strengthen their case, I was asked

Charles J. Fletcher inducted into the Aviation Hall of Fame and
Museum of New Jersey. Mrs. Herbert D. Kelleher (left),
wife of deceased husband and founder of Southwest Airlines,
and Bernice Falk Haydu (right), WASP leader and pilot during
World War II.

to be a paid consultant to review numerous depositions they planned to take of witnesses from Hovercraft, Ltd., as well as other specialists. I was still fuming over the way I had been treated by the Fort Eustis Army personnel and losing my patent rights to their security regulations regarding military inventions. Nevertheless, after more than twenty-five years, I felt it in my best interest to act as a consultant as well as to gain the possible chance of being cited as the real inventor of the multipurpose "Hovercraft."

One afternoon, another call came in from Mr. Townsend. What he told me blew my mind. "Charlie," he said, "one of our interviews at Fort Eustis revealed that after the funds for your development contract for the Glidemobile proposal failed to become available, one of the engineers who had reviewed the proposal forwarded your material to a friend of his in Canada. From there, this friend purportedly sold the Glidemobile proposal to friends in England, who formed Hovercraft, Ltd., with financing, we were told, through the British Ministry."

During my time as a Justice Department consultant, I traveled to Washington periodically to interview witnesses and read depositions, clarifying numerous technical terms for which interpretation was required. During this period, I was able to get my good friend Vic Adams on the payroll as another consultant for our cause. Vic was able to find a complete notebook at his home in Los Angeles where he worked for Lockheed. Just prior to the trial, Vic, who lived below a fairly steep embankment where he parked his car, went to get into his vehicle one morning when, for whatever reason, his brake disengaged. In an attempt to stop the vehicle, his leg got caught in the door, and the car dragged him down the hill, slamming his body into the house. Vic was killed almost instantly. This shocking news was a great loss to me, but fortunately for the Justice Department, Vic had given them his deposition about a year before his death.

It was around 1990 when we were informed that the 104 million dollar litigation reached a settlement. But the terms were that about $6 million (U.S. dollars) of the original $104 million

NEW JERSEY INVENTORS HALL OF FAME

*Founded in 1987 at New Jersey Institute of Technology
in New Jersey, the Invention State*

WHEREAS, it is the Mission of the New Jersey Inventors Hall of Fame to recognize the
achievements of inventors who have lived or worked in New Jersey, and

WHEREAS, it is the Mission of the New Jersey Inventors Hall of Fame to call national
attention to New Jersey's preeminent position in scientific research and its status as
the "Invention State," and

WHEREAS, it is the considered judgment of the Board of Trustees of the
New Jersey Inventors Hall of Fame that

CHARLES J. FLETCHER

has made extraordinary contributions to the advancement of knowledge and human welfare,

THEREFORE, be it resolved, that the above named inventor be inducted into the

INVENTORS HALL OF FAME

*IN WITNESS WHEREOF, I have affixed my name as Chairman of
the Selection Committee, this tenth day of February, 1993*

Peter A. Lewis, PE
Chairman of the Selection Committee

Preserving New Jersey's Distinguished
205-year Aeronautical Heritage

AVIATION HALL OF FAME & MUSEUM OF NEW JERSEY

400 FRED WEHRAN DRIVE, TETERBORO AIRPORT, TETERBORO, N. J. 07608 201-288-6344   Fax: 201-288-5666

September 16, 1999

Charles J. Fletcher
7 Valley Road
Sparta, NJ 07871

Dear Mr. Fletcher:

On behalf of our Board of Trustees, it gives me great pleasure to inform you of your unanimous election into the Aviation Hall of Fame & Museum of New Jersey.

Our Trustees recognize your service to our nation as a World War II Navy pilot, your creation of the first hovercraft in the world and your design of the rockets on rotor used during the Korean War.

The annual AHOF induction dinner will be held in May 2000. Those aeronautical pioneers who will be inducted with you include: Bernice Falk Haydu, a World War II WASP who, in 1971, gained military recognition for all women who flew in the service, Benjamin Cascio, a highly decorated Vietnam pilot with 700 helicopter missions and Herbert Kelleher, the founder and CEO of Southwest Airlines.

At your earliest convenience, it would be appreciated if you would send biographical information and photographs to our executive director Pat Reilly at the address above. They will be used in various publications and by the sculptor who creates our bronze inductee plaques.

Please accept my personal congratulations.

Sincerely,

Edmund Nelle Jr.
President

would be paid only because it was agreed that over a period of time British innovations were advanced by the British engineers, and a number of British changes surfaced in later years to improve the overall technical development of the Hovercraft.

For this the British were in part rewarded, but our records speak for themselves. While at Fletch-Aire Co., I was the first known person to hold an invention disclosure of the Hovercraft development concept, dating back to 1953.

From hearsay, it was said after the settlement that the Smithsonian Institute wrote a letter to Hovercraft, Ltd. suggesting they take their claim as the inventor out of the British history books. A copy of such a letter was never able to be obtained, however.

Soon word spread to several newspapers and magazines about the litigation and that I was declared the original inventor of the Hovercraft. In the January/February issue of *Inventors Digest*, an article titled "Setting the Record Straight," by Joanne Hayes, was published. Telling my story about its development, the article reported that the idea occurred to me while working as a flight test engineer at the Piasecki Helicopter Co., in Morton, Pennsylvania, in 1951, though the first Glidemobile plan was transposed into a detailed drawing on August 3, 1953, while serving in the Navy. The first British Hovercraft photos released around 1962 appeared to copy all of the key features of the Fletch-Aire Glidemobile. Construction from detailed drawings of the Fletch-Aire Glidemobile prototype was started in 1957. The first British Hovercraft using many of the Glidemobile features was built around 1960.

As several newspapers and magazines picked up on the Hovercraft settlement story, I was advised that I would be honored by induction into the New Jersey Inventors Hall of Fame. The awards ceremony took place at the New Jersey Institute of Technology (NJIT) on February 10, 1993. This honor was a great surprise for me, not knowing for a long period of twenty-nine years that it would be the United States Justice Department that would need to seek out evidence required to defend their U.S. Court case – Hovercraft Ltd. vs. U.S. Government. Because the lawsuit involved more than $104 million in claimed royalties, it was imperative that the Justice Department would have to find hard evidence to avoid paying such a ridiculous royalty. With our dated documentation, the U.S. Government had a convincing case.

The ultimate recognition came when the Discovery Channel decided to make a documentary detailing the origins of the Hovercraft, tracing the invention to my Navy work, beginning in 1951. The program editor asked me to send them a copy of the 16mm film of the first flight. This segment of film was inserted into the Discovery Channel documentary, declaring me the first known inventor. The documentary also implied that the first British military Hovercraft used the exact same inflatable skirt features and control system that ultimately made the Fletcher concept the final technological advancement, allowing the Hovercraft to become a huge success.

A final tribute to my contribution toward the development of the Hovercraft came when I received a letter in late 1999 from Mr. Edmund Nelle Jr., President of the Aviation Hall of Fame and Museum of New Jersey, announcing on behalf of their trustees, that I was going to be inducted in their Hall of Fame on May 11, 2000. This belated recognition was an award beyond my wildest dreams. When the news broke, the Sparta, New Jersey, Historical Society approached the town fathers about locating a marble memorial on the shore of the small lake where the Glidemobile was first tested and later demonstrated for the editors of *Design News*.

On May 11, 2000, with my induction into the New Jersey Aviation Hall of Fame and Museum, I was presented with a life-size oak and bronze plaque of my face and an inscription of my contribution to aviation. The plaque of my bronze "smiling face" will hang with other distinguished individuals of the aviation industry, including Charles Lindbergh and Buzz Aldrin of Montclair, New Jersey, who journeyed to the moon in 1969 with Neil Armstrong, the first human to walk on Earth's orbiting satellite. I now feel all my efforts as an aeronautical design engineer have been more than fully rewarded. As I write this, The New Jersey Aviation Hall of Fame has nominated me to the National Aviation Hall of Fame.

On June 29, 2001 the chairman of the New Jersey Budget and Appropriations Committee notified me that $25,000 was approved by the legislature for restoration of my original Hovercraft prototype that has been held over the years in storage. Upon completion of this work, the vehicle, formerly known as the "Glidemobile," will be donated to the New Jersey Aviation Hall of Fame Museum upon completion of the restoration sometime in 2002.

At this stage of my life, I still enjoy working every day, seeking some new fascination that may lead to a new product development. Each day presents a new challenge, a new opportunity in an effort to survive in the complex and increasing competitive world of American industry.

The Fletcher Family

Helen and Charles dance at their son
Jeffrey's wedding.

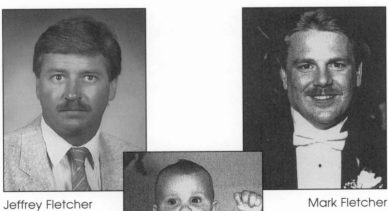

Jeffrey Fletcher   Mark Fletcher

Granddaughter Haley Marie

26

Into the Millennium

$\int$till faced with the financial obligation of the Environmental
Superfund settlement, now being finalized, I have taken positive steps addressing all our company personnel. Our message is
to focus on new and exciting technology, while always being
innovative on all fronts and aggressively pursuing an overall plan
to further our corporate desire to advance dramatically into the
21st century.

We have reorganized high-level management with talent
capable of energizing our people into believing that "Anything is
Possible." With this "Can-Do" attitude among all of our employees, specific growth goals can be achieved.

Leading the charge for Technology General is Robert J.
Tice, a brilliant engineer, designer, and machinist who owned a
manufacturing company specializing in instrumentation panels,
process control equipment, and R&D prototype systems. Bob
Tice, of nearby Stockholm, New Jersey, can literally design, engineer, and build just about anything in today's high-tech marketplace. Holder of three patents, he essentially has been a
"one-man" company leader since joining our operation in late
1999. We are beginning to see a variety of new and improved
products almost daily that both people and industry need.

To this end, we have also moved into the advanced comput-
erized managerial systems that will map out a plan for major

industrial real estate expansion coupled with new objectives for expanding sales growth of our numerous industrial products that are the backbone of our divisional corporate segments.

In realizing this dream, I hope this never-ending quest for survival will prove fruitful for all those who work at their full potential to achieve ultimate success.

My lifetime philosophy has always kept me moving forward. Some insights toward this goal include:

- Believe in yourself and what you are doing
- Listen to your intuitive voice
- Always look for the benefits of whatever task you undertake
- Every innovation, every new technology must improve the quality of life for all people and their environment
- Be of good spirit and recognize those who have done an excellent job. Genuine praise boosts morale
- Think of time as a precious human resource. Don't waste it. Make it work for you and those with whom you work
- Always be thankful for your achievements, however small. It's the collective results that count
- Always be gracious in your day-to-day dealings with people, whatever their lot in life. Corporate secretaries today can become corporate executives, and even CEOs, tomorrow
- We all live in a world of endless opportunities
- The world belongs to the doers, not the complainers or slackers
- Be a daily doer — and enjoy every minute of it
- Always pay tribute to the one who counts the most — your God

Charles J. Fletcher